DRUM WARS
— Realistic Drum Solos Unfolded —

By Carmine Appice, Vinny Appice, and Eric Fischer

For access to the digital files referenced in this book,
go to moderndrummer.com/mylibrary

Enter Code
H7Z2GP-PJ276Z-B6WMSM

Subscribe to *Modern Drummer*, the world's best drumming magazine,
at: www.moderndrummer.com/subscribe

For fun and educational videos, subscribe to the
"Modern Drummer Official" YouTube channel.

Modern Drummer Publisher/CEO **David Frangioni**

Managing Director/SVP **David Hakim**

© Copyright 2021 Modern Drummer Publications, Inc.
International Copyright Secured
All Rights Reserved
Printed in the USA

Any unauthorized duplication of this book or
its contents is a violation of copyright laws.

Published by:
Modern Drummer Publications, Inc.
1279 W Palmetto Park Rd
PO Box 276064
Boca Raton, FL 33427

Contents

Foreword 3
Acknowledgements 3
Carmine's Solo 4
   Exercises and Examples 4
      Notation Key 4
      Intro Groove 5
      Double-Bass Shuffle 9
      Triplets Between Double Bass Drums and Toms 13
      Hand and Foot Combinations 15
      Snare and China Cymbal Combinations 17
          Practice Between the Snare and Bass Drums 17
          Combinations with Triplets 18
      Stick Clicking 20
      Triplet Accents on the Snare, with Double Bass Drums Underneath 22
      Three-Stroke Ruffs 28
      Triplets with the China Cymbals, Toms, and Bass Drums 30
   Carmine's Complete Drum Solo Transcription 32
Vinny's Solo 40
   Exercises and Examples 40
      Notation Key 40
      Intro Groove 40
      Snare Drum Patterns 42
Triplets Between the Toms and Bass Drum 44
      Triplet Ruffs 45
      Sixteenth-Note Groove 46
      Groups of Seven-Note Combinations 48
      Paradiddles Around the Drumset 49
      Groups of Six-Note Combinations 50
      Groove with Thirty-Second Notes 51
   Vinny's Complete Drum Solo Transcription 53

Foreward

The concept of this book and video is to take drum solos of me and my brother, Vinny Appice, and break them down into easily digestible sections. By viewing the included video footage of the solos at 75% and 50% of the normal speed, the student can see and hear each section at an understandable speed. With the addition of MIDI audio, each solo is presented with the clearest sound, even at the slower speeds. A complete transcription of each solo is also included for the reading student.

The beauty of this book and video is that each section of the solos includes explanations to help students learn what is being played on the video. Also included are a number of foundation patterns that will help the student learn the recorded solo patterns slowly, as written out by me and my co-writer, Eric Fischer.

I think young student drummers will love *Drum Wars*—it will help teach them **how to build a drum solo** (which, deep down inside, we all want to do). As a kid starting out, I would record solos by my favorite drummers on my tape machine at high speed. I would then play these solos back at a slower speed so I could hear them with as much detail as possible. In those days, this was a great way to learn solos. This book and video package now takes this concept to the next level. Its modern approach teaches through the use of various mediums, including the visual, audio, and written examples.

This comprehensive approach should prove to be fun and instructional.

—Carmine Appice

From the Publisher

Carmine Appice is a true drumming legend. Carmine was not only one of rock's first drum heroes, he was also an inspiration to me as a child. The moment I picked up Realistic Rock, I was hooked! (I subsequently collected all of his books, but Realistic Rock was my first Carmine drum book.)

I remember that it had a picture of Carmine's double-bass maple drumkit with a gong drum over the floor toms, double China cymbals upside down, electronic drums above the rack toms…I could go on and on. I was inspired, and I hadn't even opened the book yet! Once inside this treasure trove of rock rhythms and concepts, I found a virtually endless vocabulary available from which to draw new ideas and to perfect the important, solid playing that every drummer needs to know.

The benefit of working through Carmine's catalog is that it improves your playing quickly. You will save enormous amounts of time by practicing his exercises. This is the formula to fast-track your rock drumming prowess!

Modern Drummer is proud to present the entire Carmine Appice catalog, which to this day still inspires our playing! Enjoy, and we wish you the best always on your drumming journey.

David Frangioni
CEO/Publisher of Modern Drummer Publications, Inc.

Acknowledgements

Carmine would like to thank ddrum Signature Products, Vic Firth Signature Sticks, Sabian Signature Cymbals, Evans Drumheads, Audix Mics, DW Pedals and Hardware, Canopus Products, Puresound Snare Wires, Calzone/Anvil Cases, Zoom Products, and Gator Cases.

Vinny would like to thank Joey Wester, Istanbul Mehmet Cymbals, ddrum, Vic Firth Sticks, Gator Cases, and Evans Drumheads. Special thanks to Elliot Rubinson.

Eric would like to thank Carmine and Vinny, Dave Black, Carl Palmer, Bruce Pilato, Michael Parillo, *Modern Drummer Magazine*, Melissa Fischer, Lily and Sophie Fischer, Tom Starr, and Bill Cairo.

CARMINE'S SOLO
Exercises and Examples

Notation Key

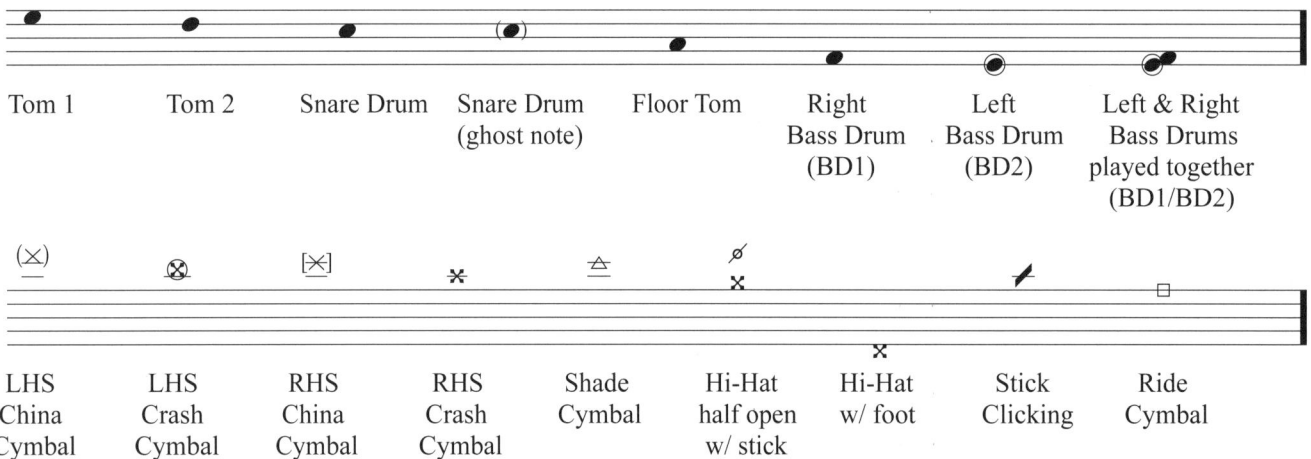

Before introducing the Groove of Carmine's solo, here's a quick explanation of how the notation is used throughout.

The "L" and "R" denote sticking for the hands only. The feet have their dedicated positions on the staff that indicate right or left foot (BD1 and BD2, respectively). The examples below show two ways in which the sticking for the hands can be notated. They are played exactly the same.

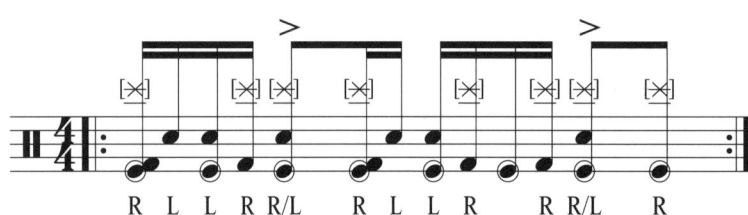

The example above is the same as the one below.

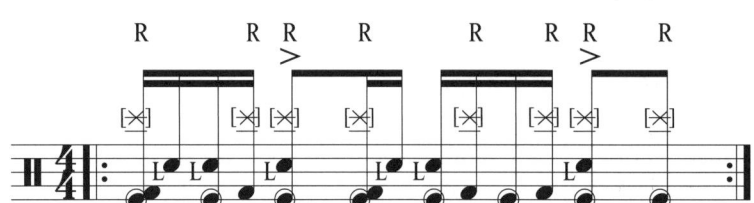

INTRO GROOVE

This section begins at 19:57 (100% normal speed), at 13:52 (75% of the normal speed), and at 4:50 (50% of the normal speed).

The basic groove consists of eighth notes on the half-open hi-hat, a syncopated bass drum, and the snare on beats 2 and 4.

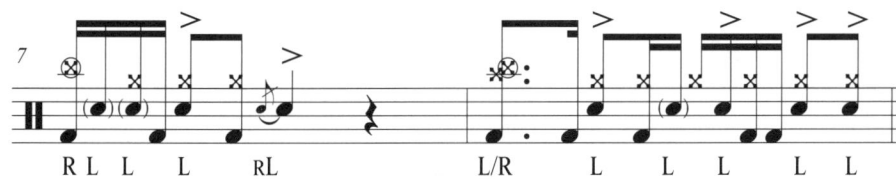

Adding ghost notes on the snare drum creates the following pattern.

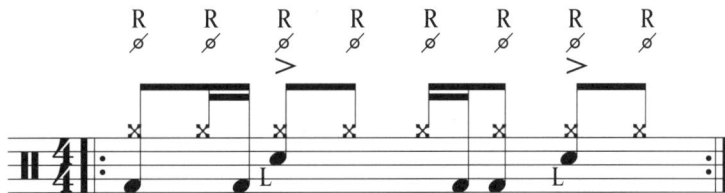

The ghost notes make up a pattern of sixteenth notes played among the snare, hi-hat, and bass drum, and should be counted as such.

Each set of four sixteenths is equal to one quarter note.

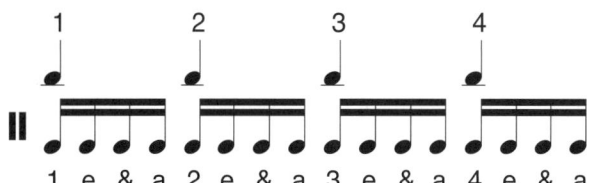

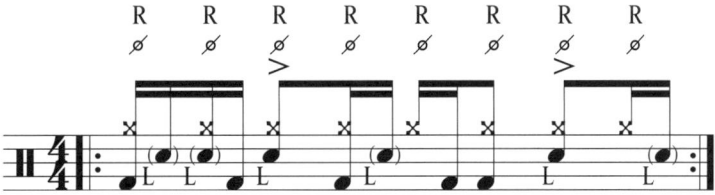

6 DRUM WARS | CARMINE'S SOLO

This groove builds into the following phrase based on sixteenth notes.

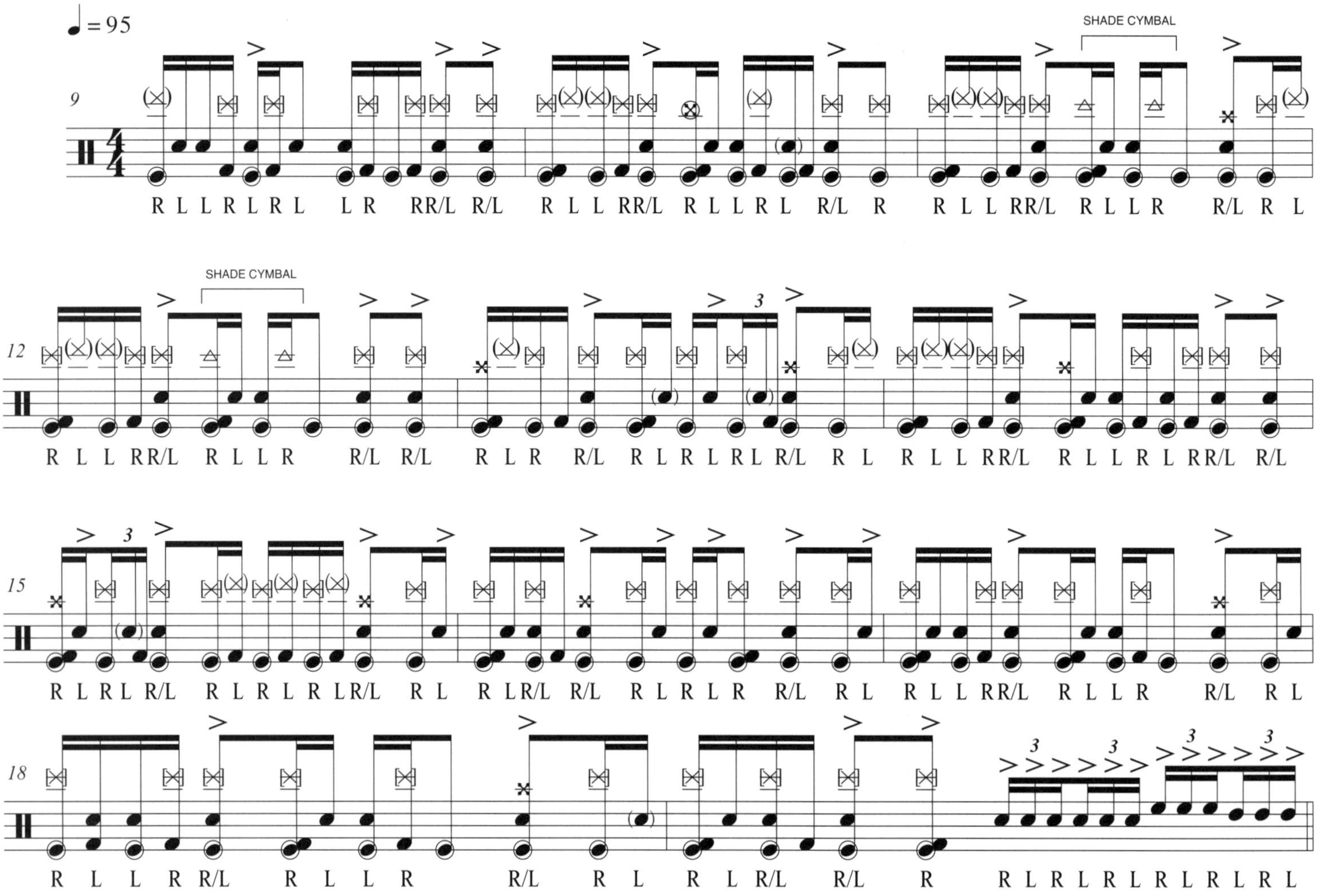

[Sheet music: measures 9–20, ♩=95, 4/4 time, with sticking notation R/L below each note and "SHADE CYMBAL" markings above certain passages]

To help develop this groove, start with the following pattern using the snare drum, and the China cymbal on the right-hand side.

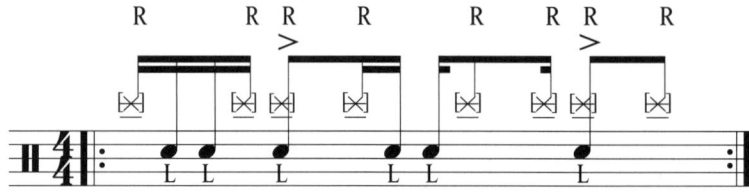

Now add the right bass drum to produce the following pattern.

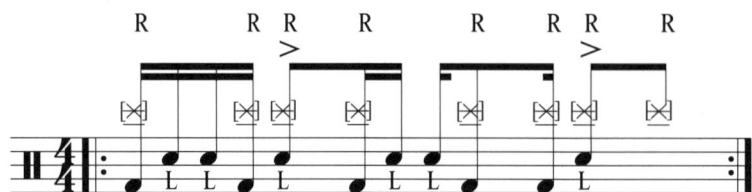

Start slowly at first, and repeat this groove as you continue to build up speed.

To practice independence, now add quarter notes played with the left bass drum. The goal is to eventually play eighth notes on the left bass drum against the other three limbs.

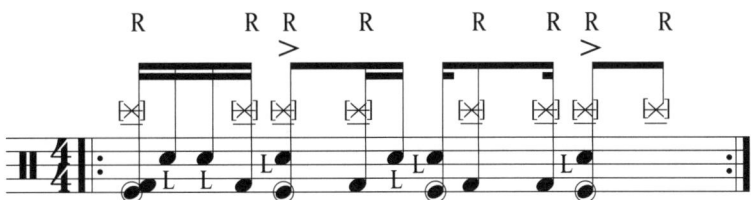

Here is an example of playing only the left bass drum on the "&" of each beat.

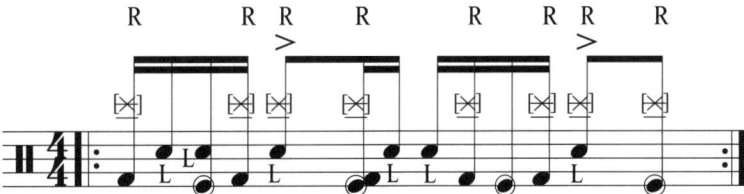

Finally, playing all eighth notes on the left bass drum creates the following groove of alternating sixteenth notes on both bass drums on beat 3.

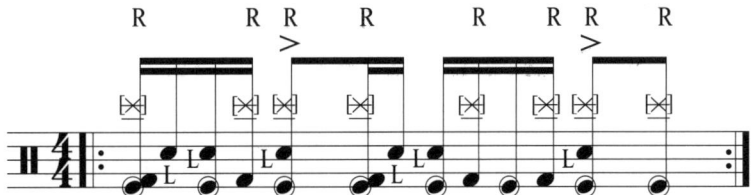

Remember, start slowly and build up to the transcription speed on the video and MP3s.

The final element needed to play this groove is to move the left hand to the China cymbal on the left-hand side, and play it on the "e-&" of beat 1.

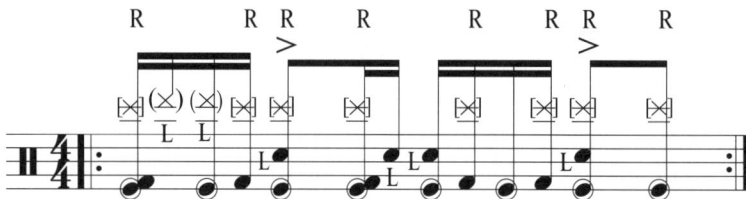

Below are two variations of the groove that appear in the transcription.

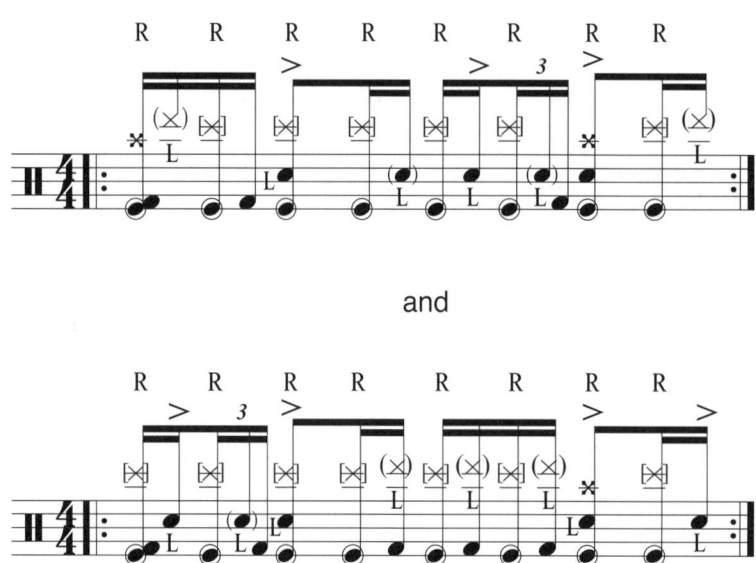

As you can see, both of these variations involve eighth notes placed on the left bass drum. Pay close attention to the China-cymbal rhythms on the left-hand side.

DOUBLE-BASS SHUFFLE

This section begins at 20:44 (100% normal speed), at 14:54 (75% of the normal speed), and at 6:23 (50% of the normal speed).

At slower tempos, the shuffle rhythm is typically notated using triplets. At faster tempos, the rhythm may be notated using eighth notes, as it tends to "even out" at faster tempos. The following exercises are notated using triplets, and should be practiced at slower tempos. Later in the book, the same exercises will appear again (written as eighth notes) to show how the rhythms evolve at faster tempos.

In each of the following exercises, the quarter notes are played on the right-hand China cymbal.

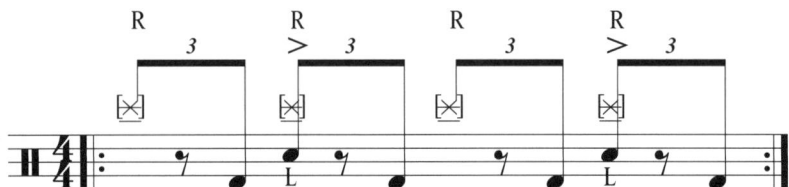

Now let's add the left bass drum on beat 1.

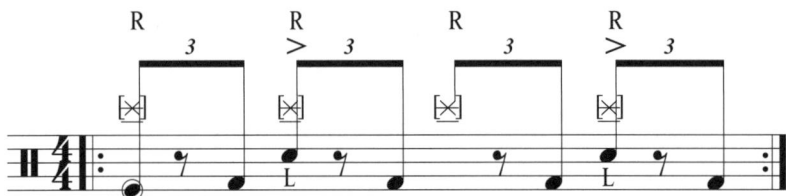

Now let's add the left bass drum on beat 3.

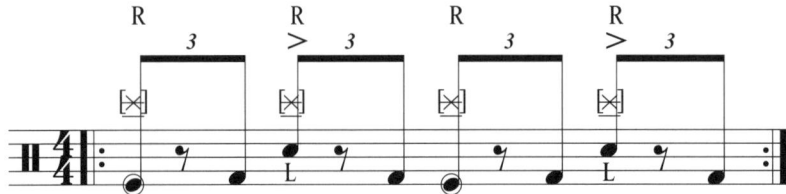

Finally, let's add the left bass drum on all four beats. This will produce the double-bass shuffle!

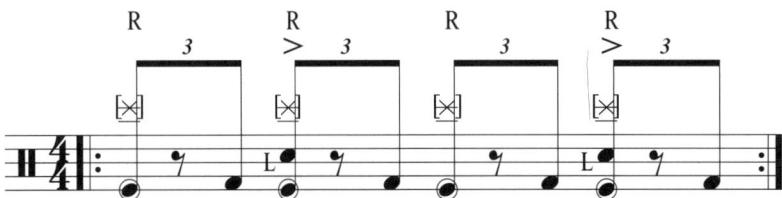

Remember to start slowly and gradually build up to speed!

Adding the following ghost notes on the snare creates a quarter-note triplet feel over the double bass-drum shuffle.

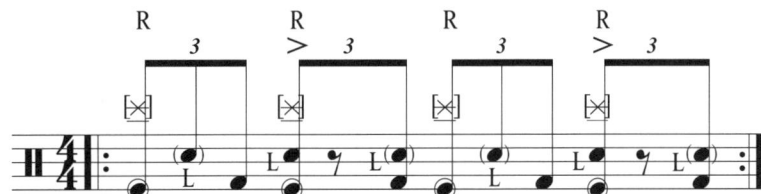

By starting the quarter-note triplet on the last partial of beat 1, the backbeat will land on beat 3. This gives the groove a half-time feel.

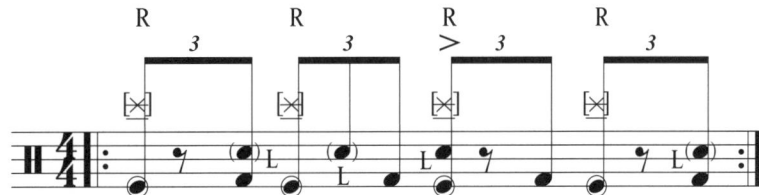

Moving the quarter-note triplets around the toms will give us the following pattern.

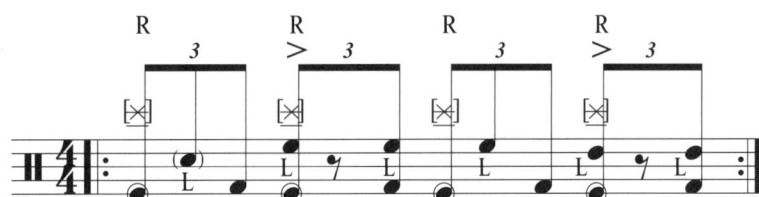

This, then, leads us to the following pattern from the transcription. Initially, it can be practiced in 3/4 time.

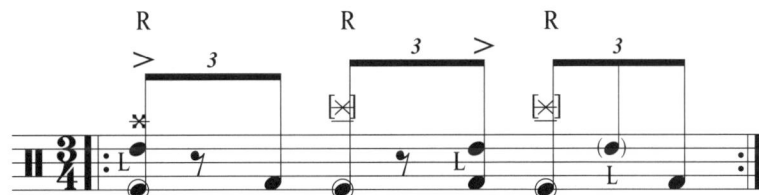

The pattern repeats in the transcription. Now written in 4/4 time, it has a "2 over 3" polyrhythmic feel and resolves after three measures.

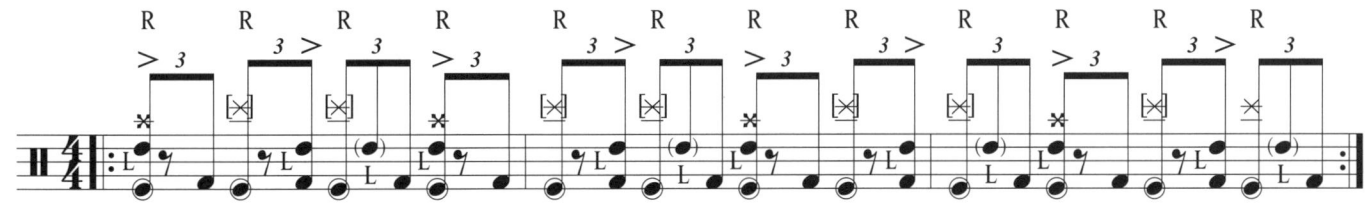

As mentioned in this section, shuffle-based rhythms can be written as eighth notes at faster tempos. The following exercises sound the same as the previous ones from this section, except they are now voiced as eighth notes.

Ghost Notes over the Double-Bass Groove

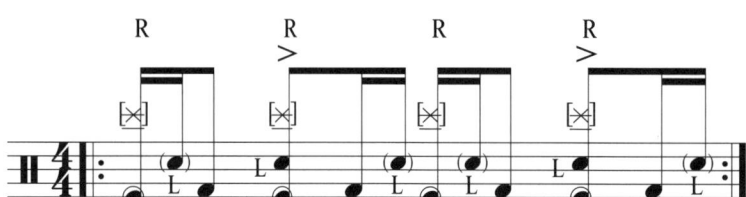

Moving the Left Hand Around the Toms

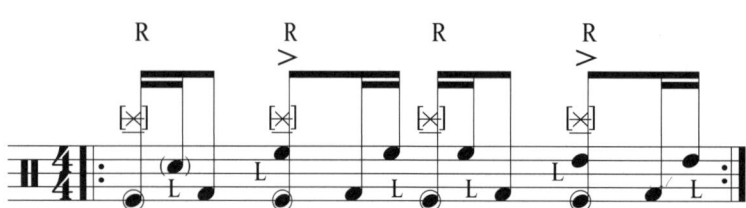

Half-Time Feel

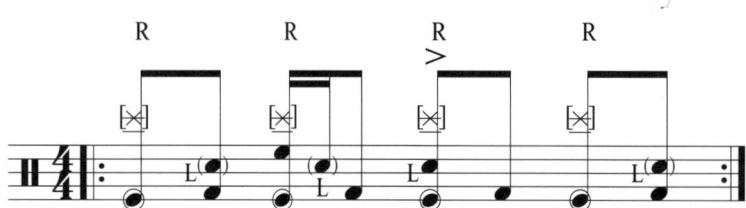

"2 over 3" Polyrhythm

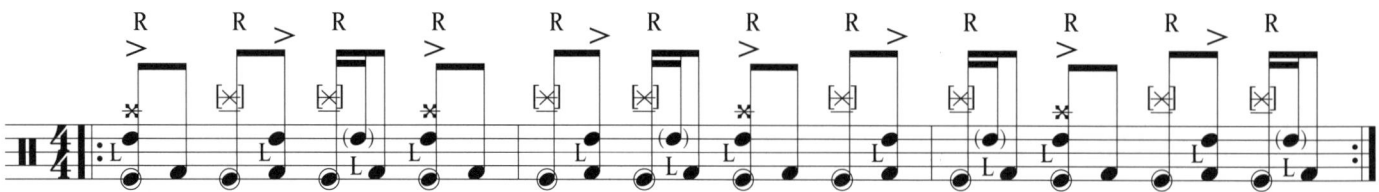

Please refer to the full transcription to see how these patterns blend together.

TRIPLETS BETWEEN DOUBLE BASS DRUMS AND TOMS

This section begins at 21:04 (100% normal speed), at 15:20 (75% of the normal speed), and at 7:01 (50% of the normal speed.

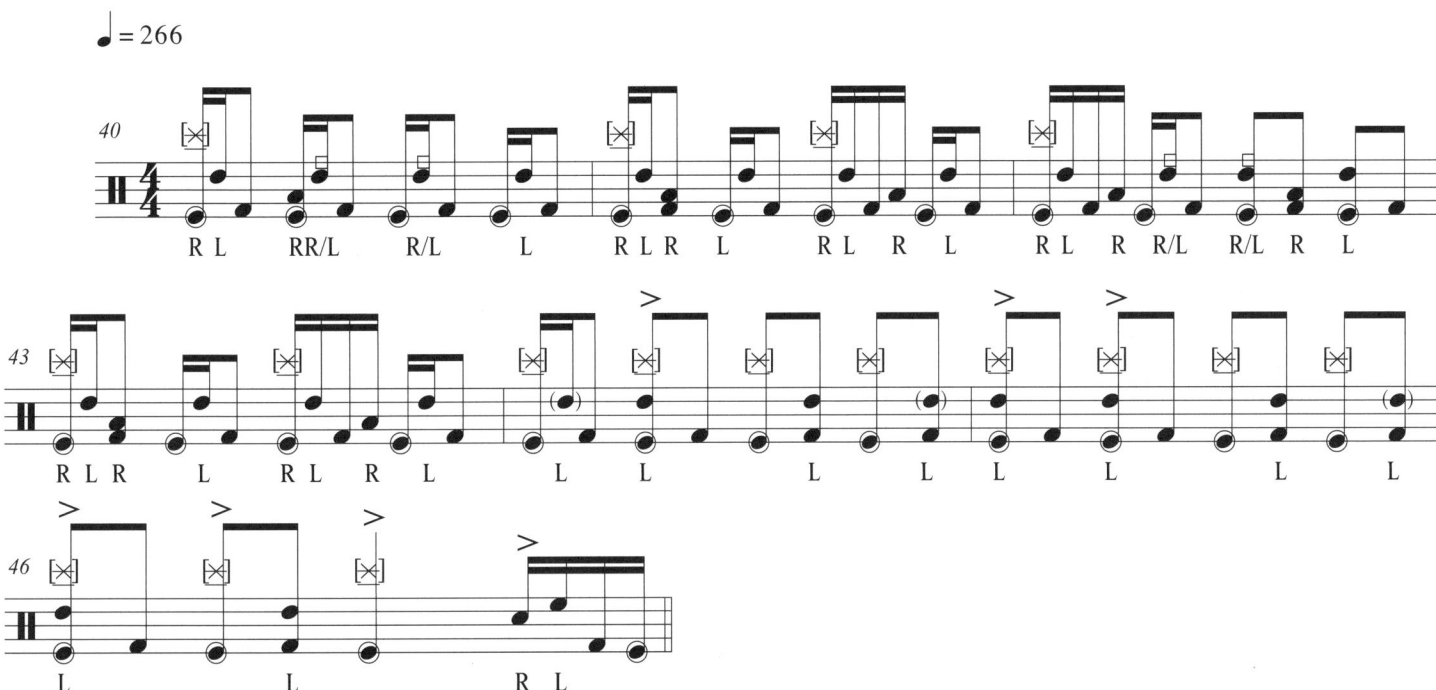

Because the triplet rhythm tends to "even out" at faster tempos, the transcription has been notated using eighth notes. However, as stated earlier, at slower tempos the shuffle rhythm is typically notated using triplets. The following exercises, which should be practiced at slower tempos, have been notated using triplets.

The following pattern allows you to create triplets by inserting the left hand within the double bass drum-shuffle rhythm. As you can see, the left bass drum plays with the right hand. Start with your right hand on the China cymbal. Your left hand will play on the tom, followed by your right foot (which completes the triplet on beat 1).

Adding the right and left hands on beat 2 will result in the following beat.

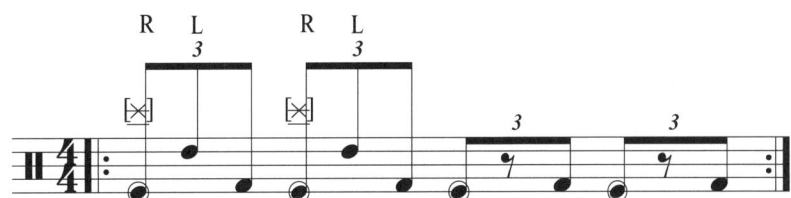

You can build up the phrase by including triplets on the first three beats.

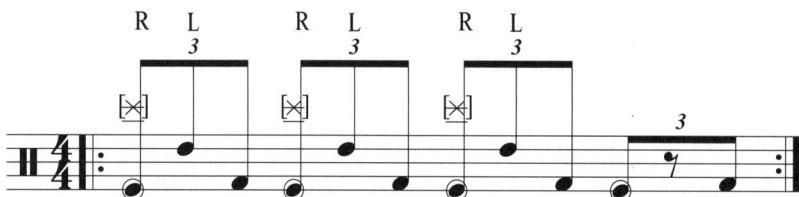

Now play triplets on all four beats. Remember to start slowly!

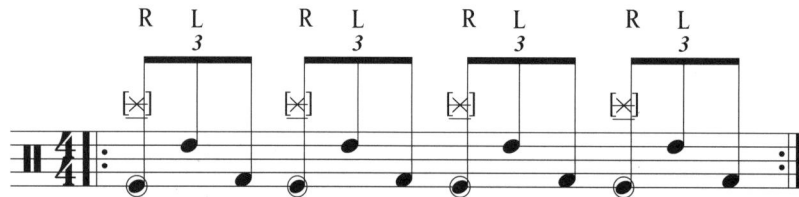

Moving your right hand between the China cymbal and floor tom will give you the following pattern. Start slowly, and work up to speed!

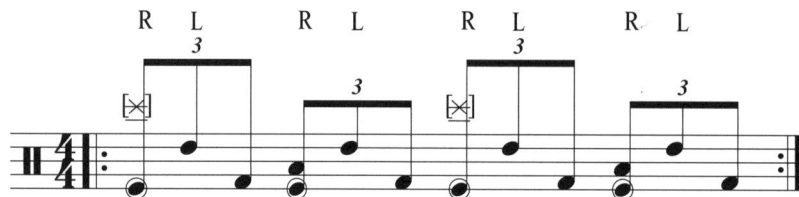

At faster tempos the triplets evolve into two sixteenths and an eighth, creating a stuttering effect.

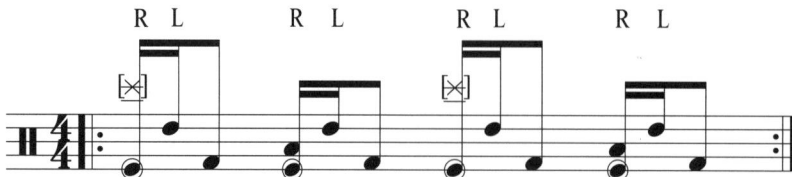

Please refer to the full transcription to see how these patterns flow into one another.

HAND AND FOOT COMBINATIONS

This section begins at 21:09 (100% normal speed), at 15:27 (75% of the normal speed), and at 7:12 (50% of the normal speed).

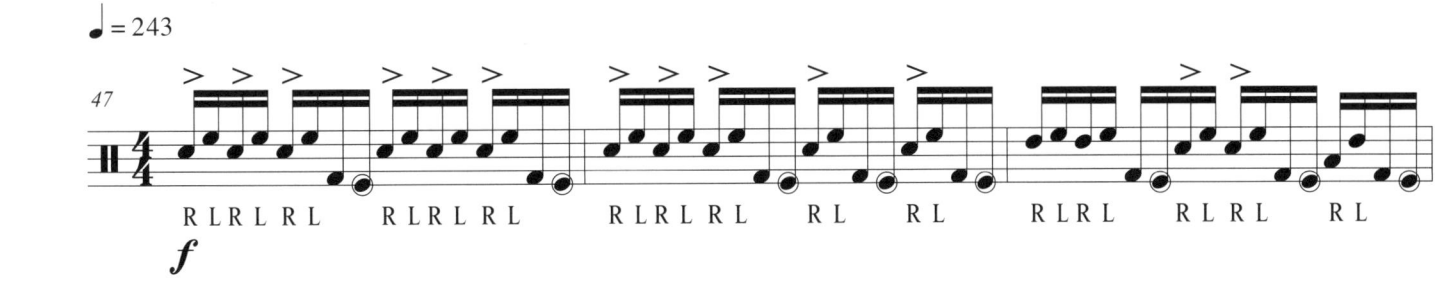

To prepare you for this section, we suggest you start with the following combination of the snare, small tom, and bass drums. Pay careful attention to the stickings, and play with an even and steady flow. Practice slowly at first in order to build up speed. Repeat over and over!

The following practice pattern includes four sixteenths played with the hands, followed by two sixteenths played with the feet. It repeats in one measure of 4/4 and resolves with two sixteenths in both the hands and feet on beat 4. Again, pay close attention to the sticking.

16 DRUM WARS I CARMINE'S SOLO

Now play six sixteenth notes with the hands, followed by sexteenth notes on the right and left bass drums. Remember to pay attention to the stickings.

Combining all these ideas now gives us the complete passage from the solo transcription. Please note that the hands move around to play the snare, tom-toms, and floor tom.

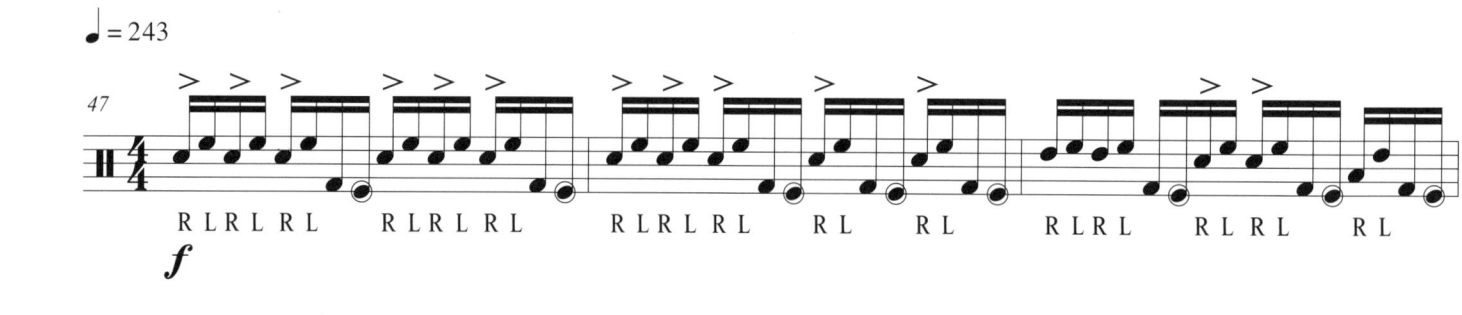

With each of these patterns, you must take your time and practice them slowly in order to build up to speed.

SNARE AND CHINA CYMBAL COMBINATIONS

This section begins at 21:59 (100% normal speed), at 16:34 (75% of the normal speed), and at 8:53 (50% of the normal speed).

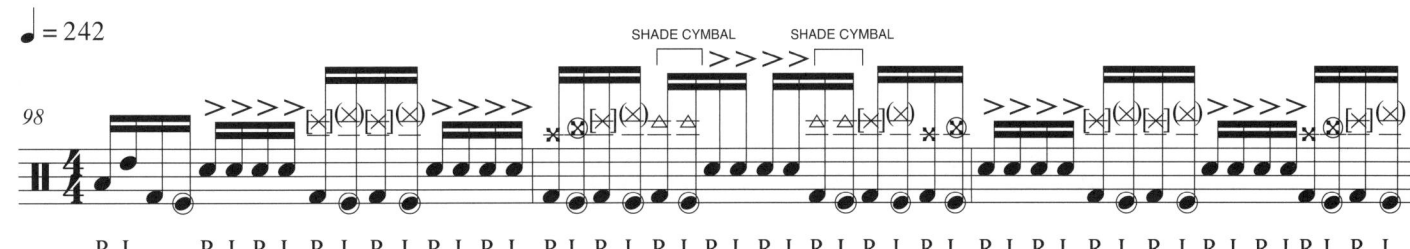

The combination exercises below are played with the hands on the snare and the two China cymbals. The China cymbals are to be played with the bass drums. As you gradually increase the speed, the short "staccato" sound of the China cymbals will help the momentum so you're able to play patterns as fast and as clean as possible.

To become comfortable with the following patterns, we recommend you first learn to play them between the snare and the double bass drums, and then gradually introduce the China cymbals.

Practice Between the Snare and Bass Drums

Play all sixteenth notes as even strokes.

18   DRUM WARS I CARMINE'S SOLO

Play these exercises slowly at first, and then build up speed. After you become comfortable, practice playing the hands and feet together with the China cymbals.

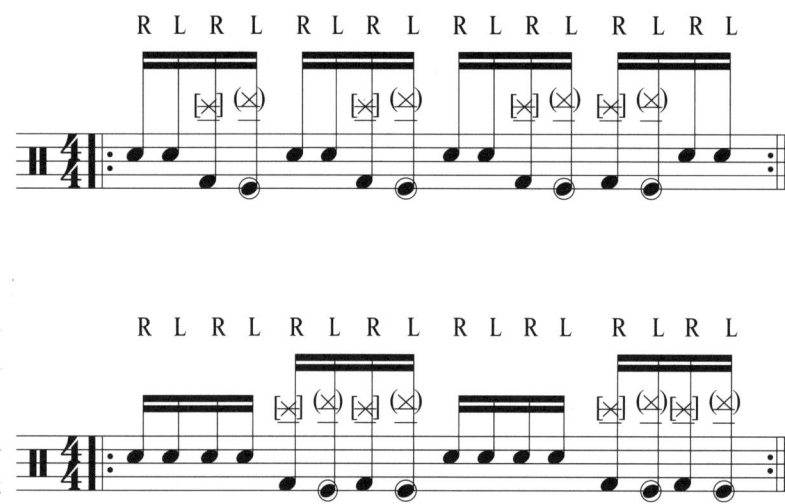

Combinations with Triplets

Make sure the triplets are played evenly. Practice slowly at first, and then gradually build up speed.

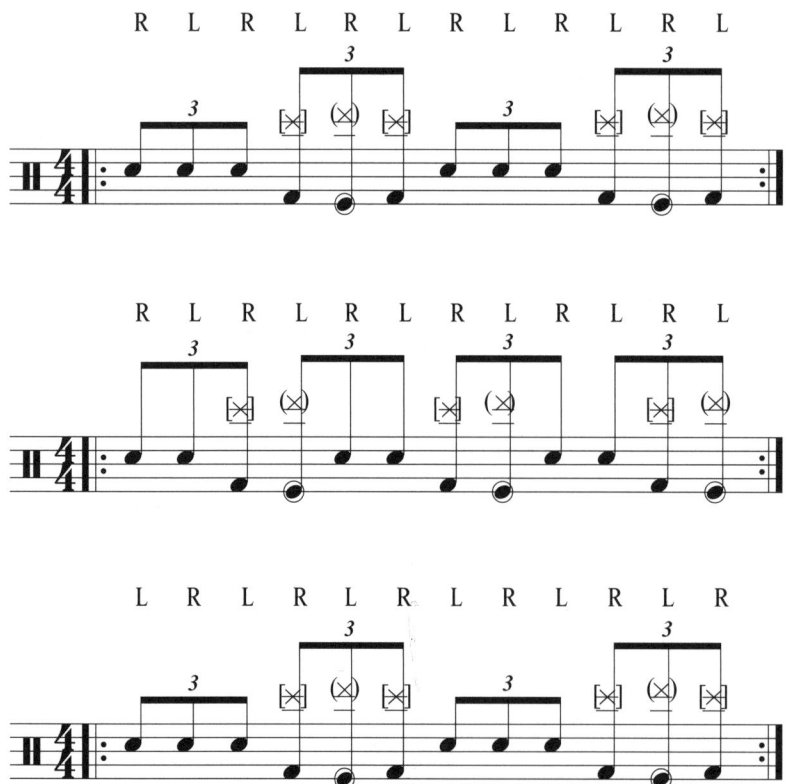

Once comfortable with all the patterns, you are ready to combine them into the section from the transcription.

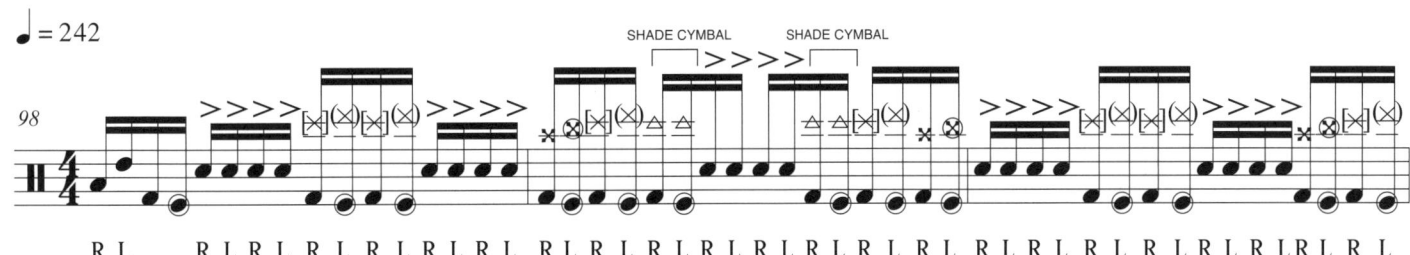

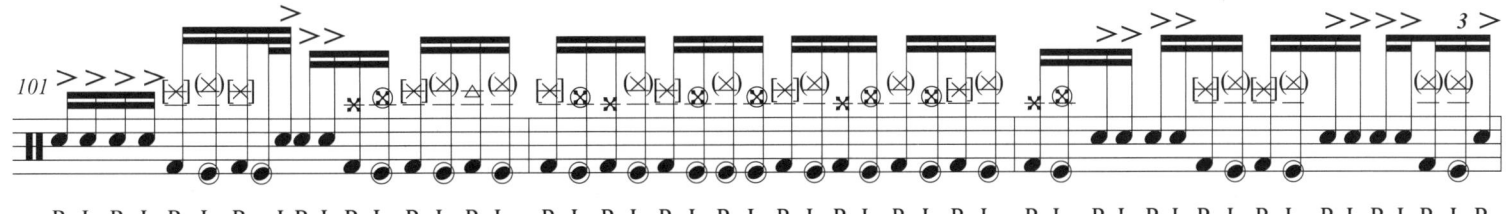

Remember to practice slowly, and then gradually build up speed!

STICK CLICKING

This section begins at 22:47 (100% normal speed), at 17:38 (75% of the normal speed), and 10:28 (50% of the normal speed.

Please refer to the video chapter on Stick Clicking to view Carmine demonstrating this technique.

To perform these patterns, hold the right drumstick with the back end out (matched grip), while stricking the left drumstick (held using traditional grip). The back end of the right stick will strike downward toward the left drumstick. The tip of the right drumstick strikes the left drumstick with an upward motion. For a more detailed explanation, please refer to the video.

Here are some additional exercises to try.

Single-Stroke Roll

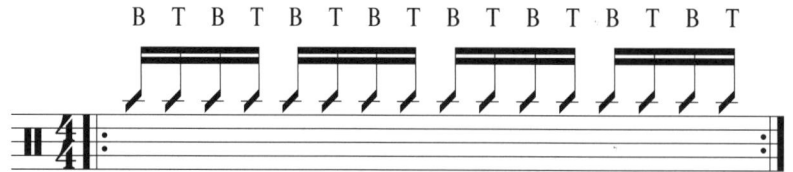

Double Strokes

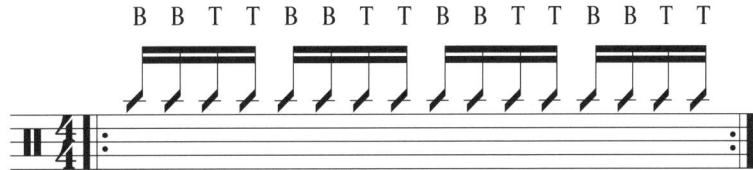

Single Paradiddle

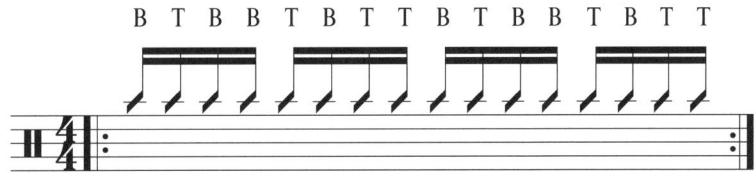

Double Paradiddle (Written in 6/4 to Be Repeated)

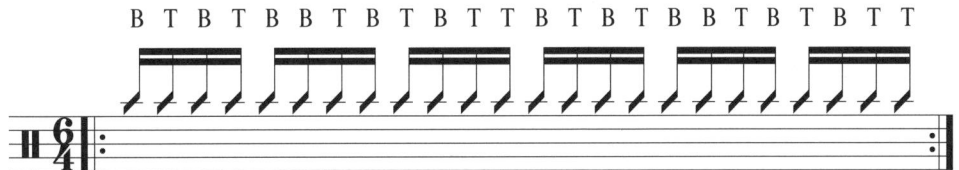

Triple Paradiddle

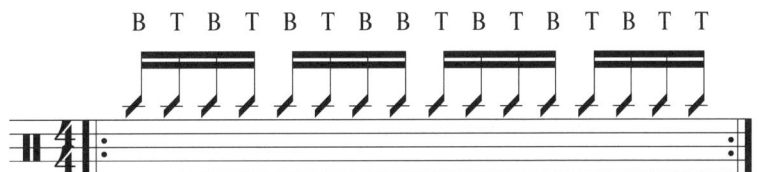

Inverted Paradiddle

Three-Stroke Ruffs

Be patient, and remember to start slowly and gradually work up to speed.

22 DRUM WARS | CARMINE'S SOLO

TRIPLET ACCENTS ON THE SNARE, WITH DOUBLE BASS DRUMS UNDERNEATH

This section begins at 23:12 (100% normal speed), at 18:10 (75% of the normal speed), and at 11:17 (50% of the normal speed.

This passage consists primarily of sixteenth-note triplets played on the snare drum. They are counted as such.

Two groups of sixteenth-note triplets equal two eighth notes.

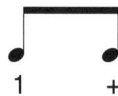

In order to play this section with the accents and double bass drums, we recommend you start with the following pattern on just the snare drum.

Start slowly and evenly, and gradually build up speed.

The following exercises should be strongly accented where indicated. Rim shots may also be used. To further enhance your facility, you may want to play all accented notes on the toms.

DRUM WARS | CARMINE'S SOLO

26 DRUM WARS | CARMINE'S SOLO

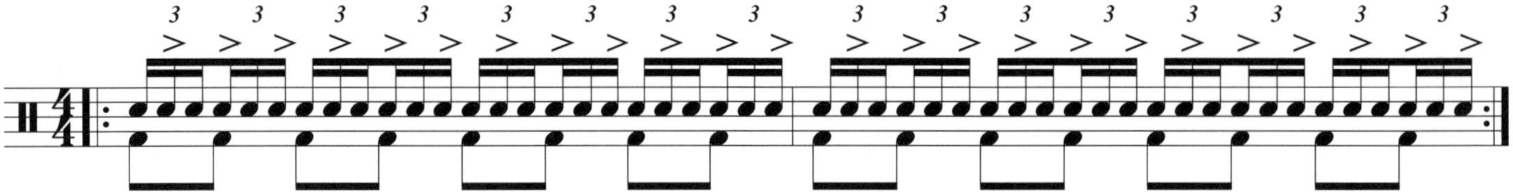

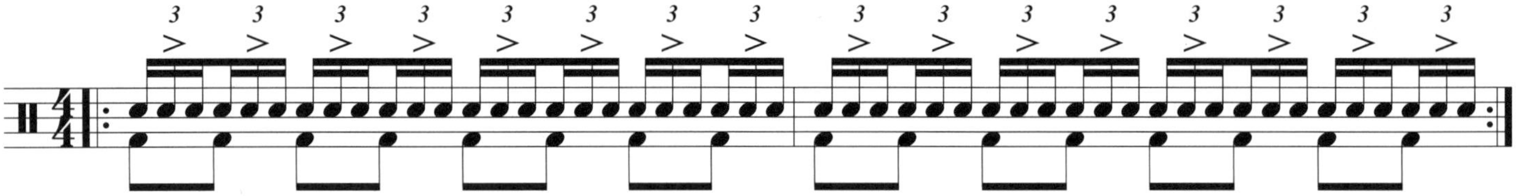

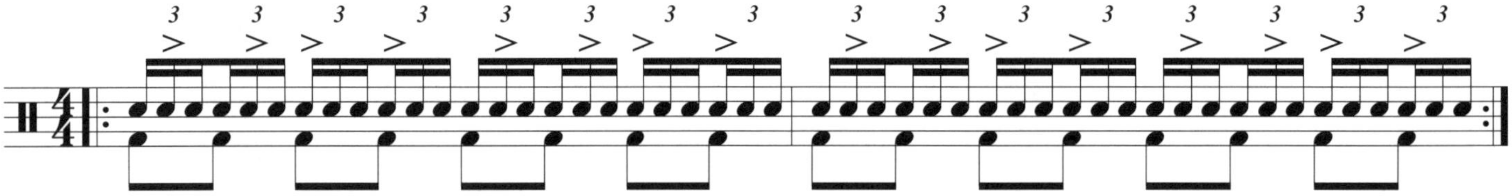

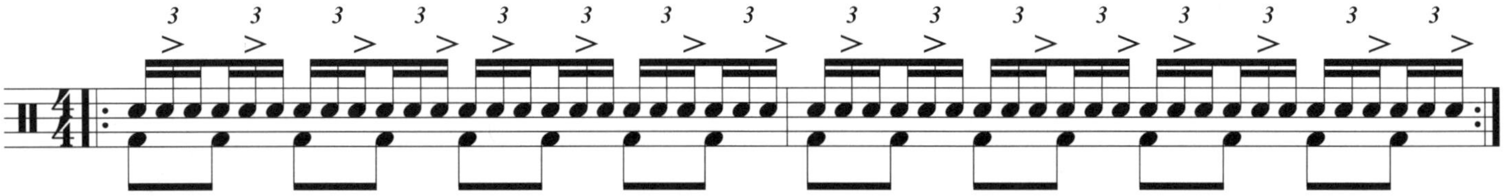

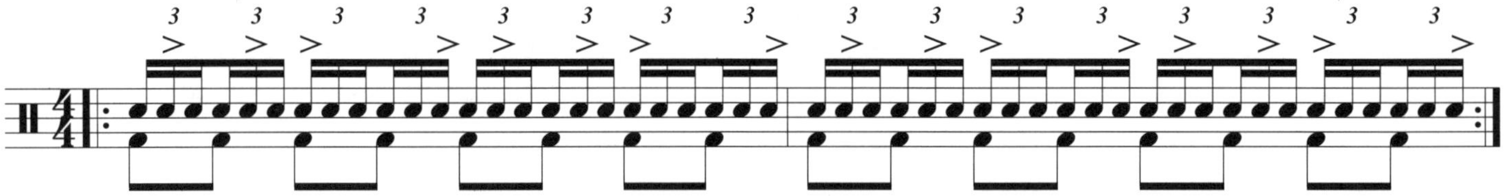

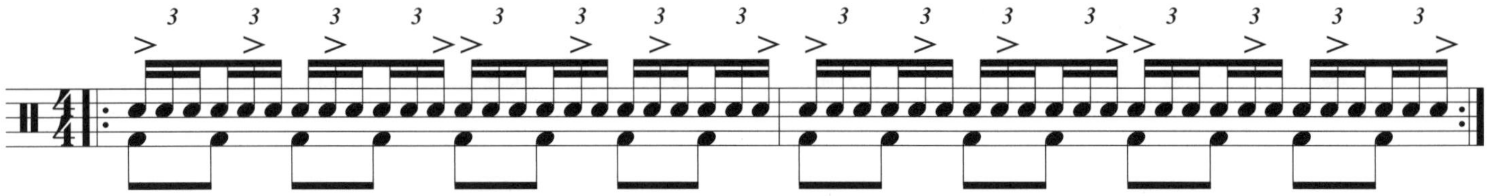

The following example is the accented snare part from the solo transcription. The previous accent studies should have prepared you for playing this section with the required dynamics.

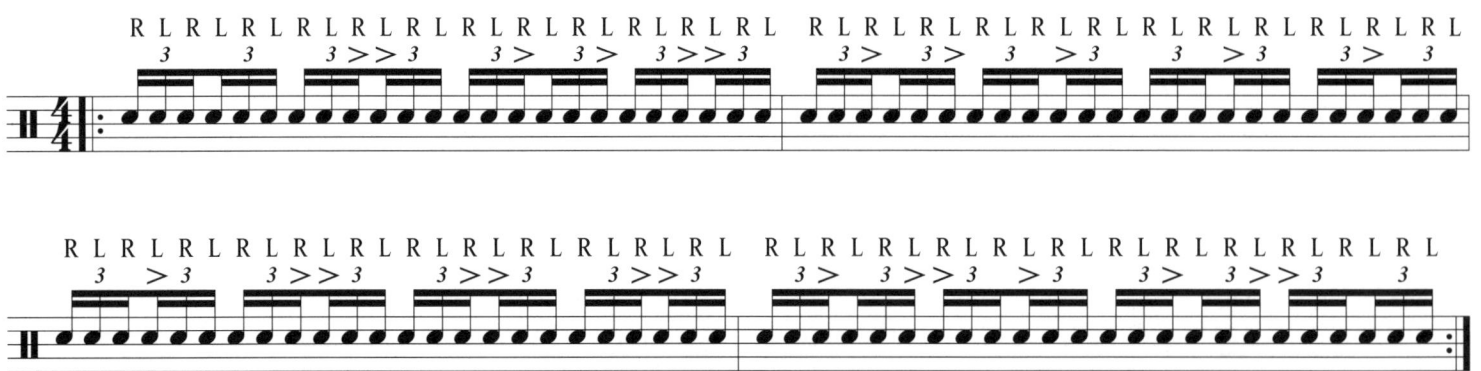

DRUM WARS | CARMINE'S SOLO

Once the accents have been mastered, add the right bass drum.

Adding the left bass drum to the pattern completes the phrase.

The left bass drum is played just after the right bass drum is stuck. The time signature in the last measure is $\frac{5}{8}$, meaning there are five eighth notes in one measure, as opposed to eight eighth notes in one measure of $\frac{4}{4}$. Count "1, 2, 3, 4 5," with each eighth note recieving one beat.

The additional markings (>) are accents to be played with less emphasis than the standard accent.

THREE-STROKE RUFFS

This section begins at 23:35 (100% normal speed), at 18:42 (75% of the normal speed), and at 12:04 (50% of the normal speed.

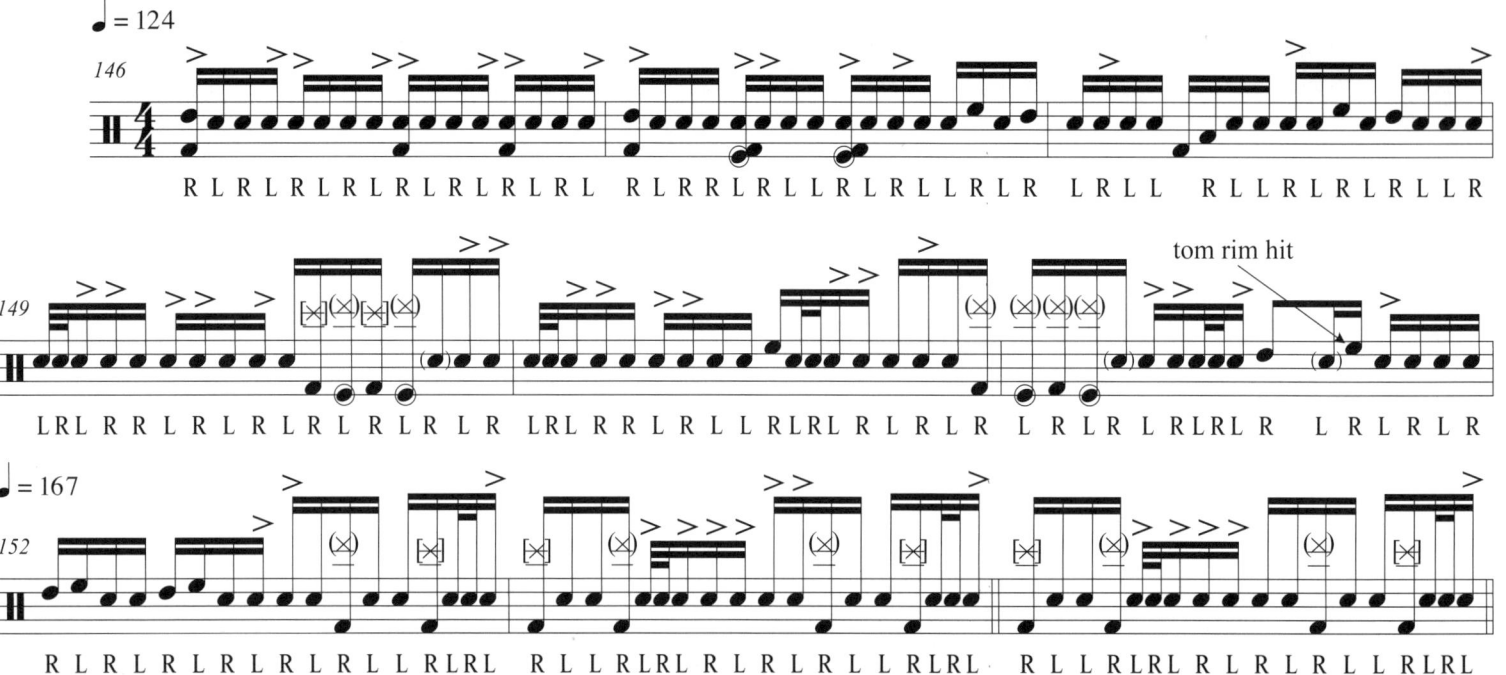

The following exercises will help develop your hands and make the three-stroke ruffs from the solo transcription easier to play. Note that there are three sticking variations. Be sure to practice each version with equal devotion. Remember to maintain a very steady tempo and observe all accents faithfully.

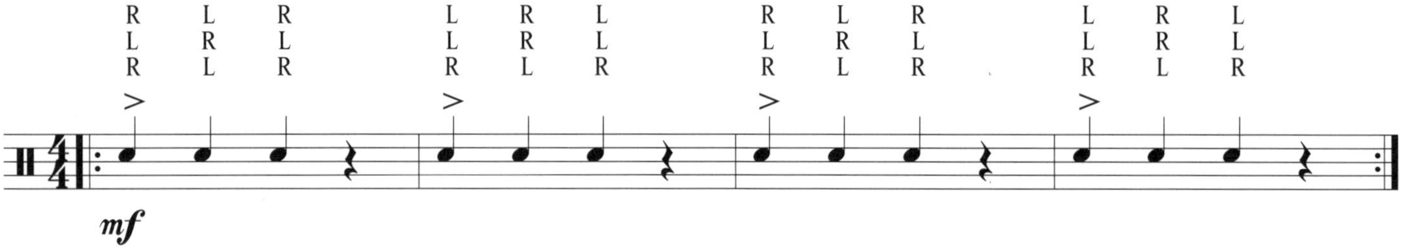

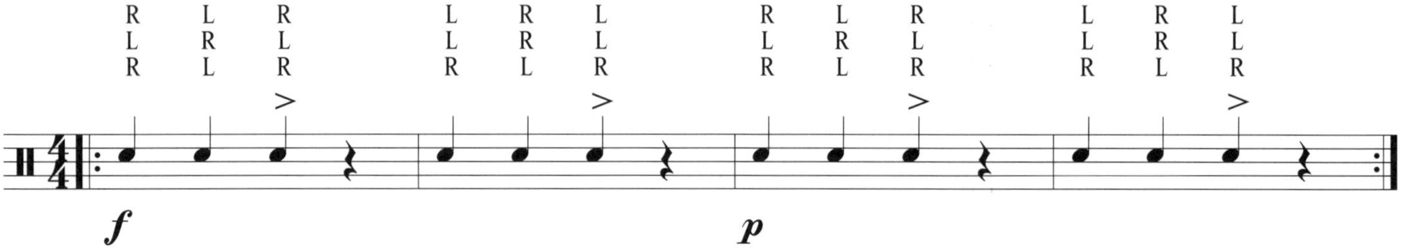

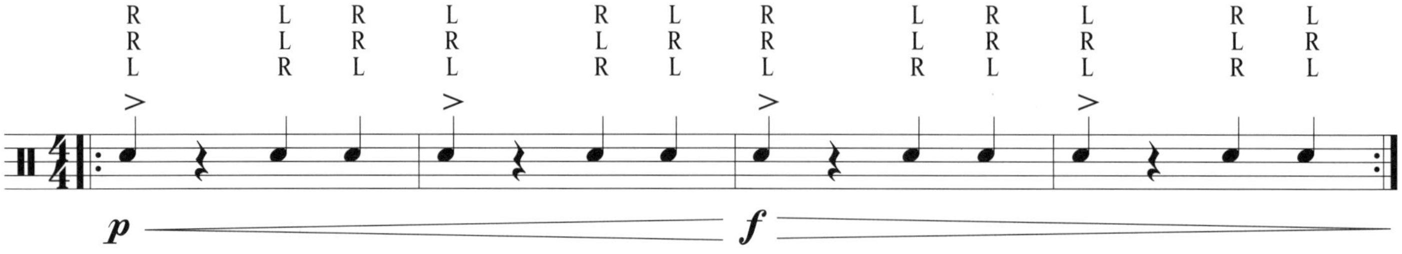

The following exercises incorporate changing dynamics and shifting accents.

TRIPLETS WITH THE CHINA CYMBALS, TOMS, AND BASS DRUMS

This section begins at 24:07 (100% normal speed), at 19:24 (75% of the normal speed), and at 13:07 (50% of the normal speed).

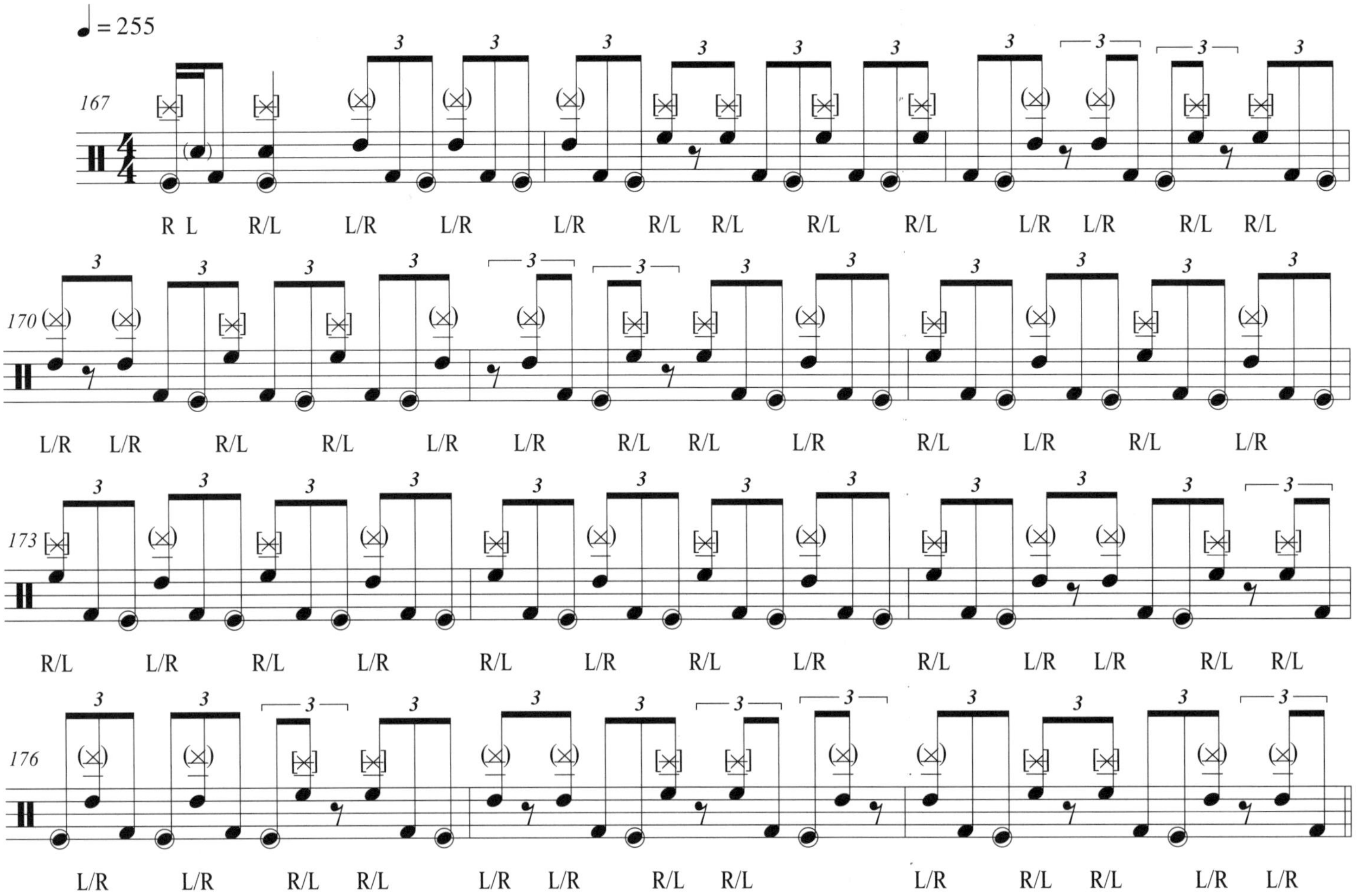

In order to develop this impressive lick, begin with the right hand on the China cymbal and the left hand on the first tom. The hands play the first note of the eighth-note triplet together, with the right and left bass drums playing the remaining two notes. Play the triplets for one full measure, as shown in the exercise below. Take your time and play the pattern evenly.

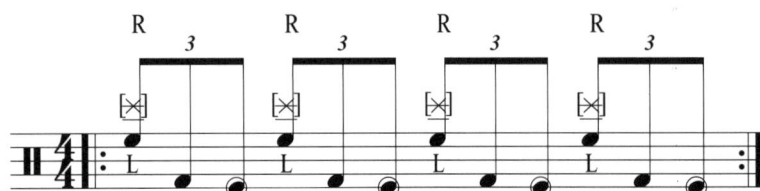

Now play the pattern by starting with the left hand on the China cymbal and the right hand on the second tom.

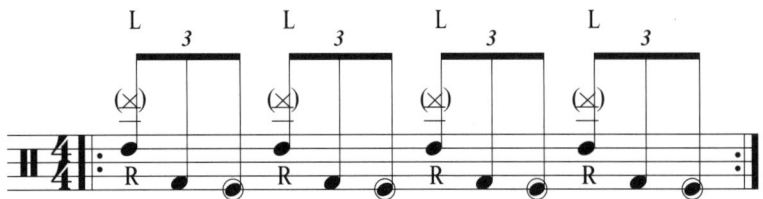

Alternating between the left- and right-hand lead helps to develop facility.

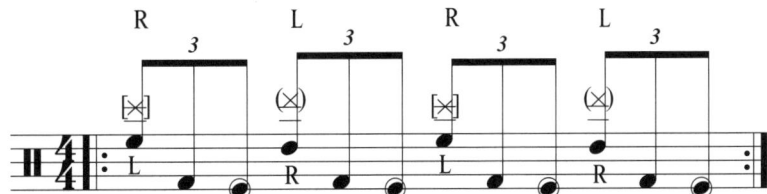

Now break up the rhythm and play two hand hits (separated by a rest in between). This will effectually turn the pattern around.

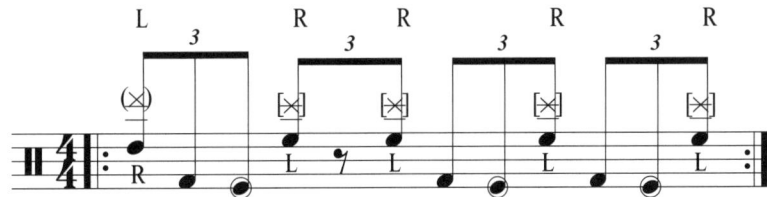

Here's a two-measure phrase of the same effect. Experiment and have fun with the many possibilities of this pattern.

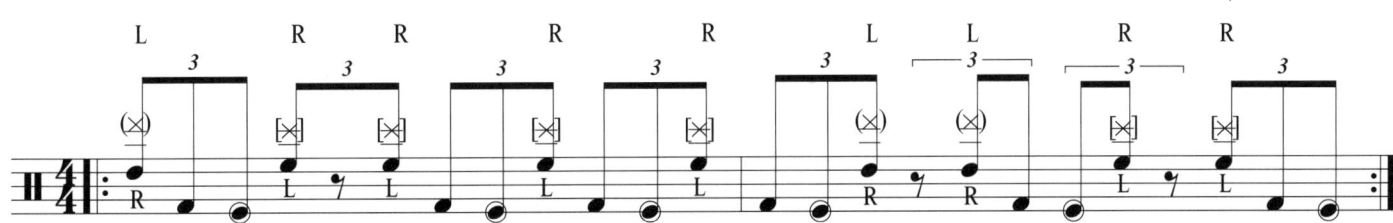

Carmine's Complete Drum Solo Transcription

Recorded Live with Cactus in 2006

Before playing the following solo, please refer to the notation legend on page 4

Transcribed by Eric Fischer

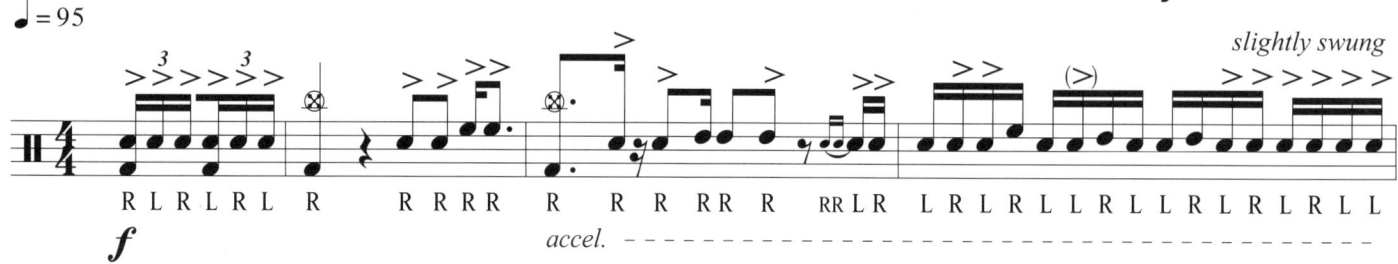

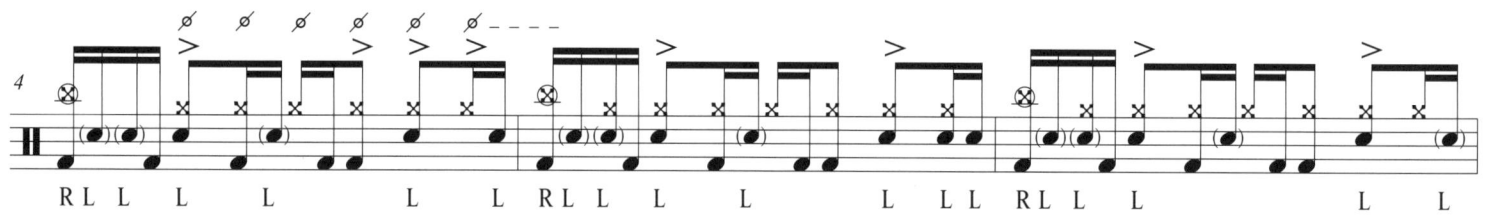

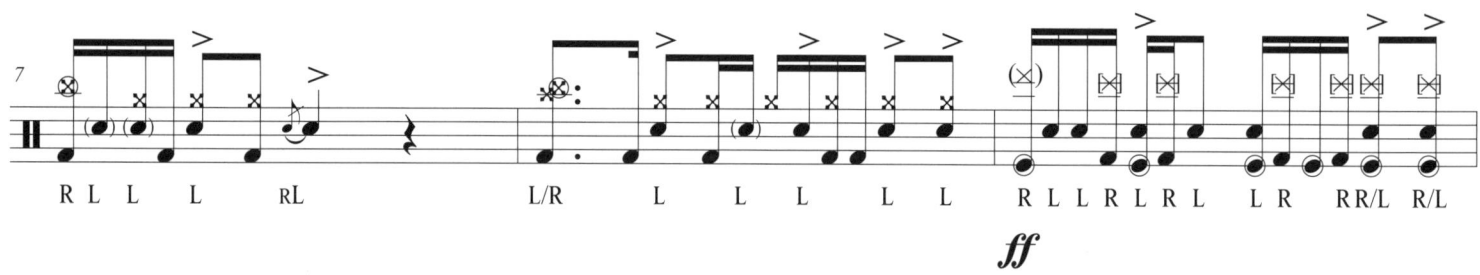

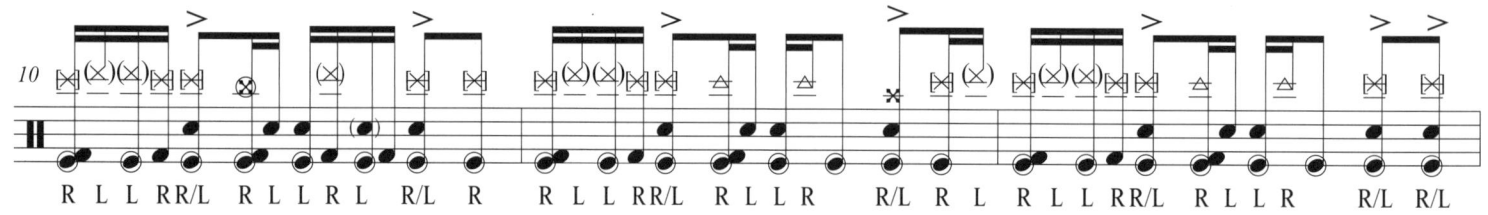

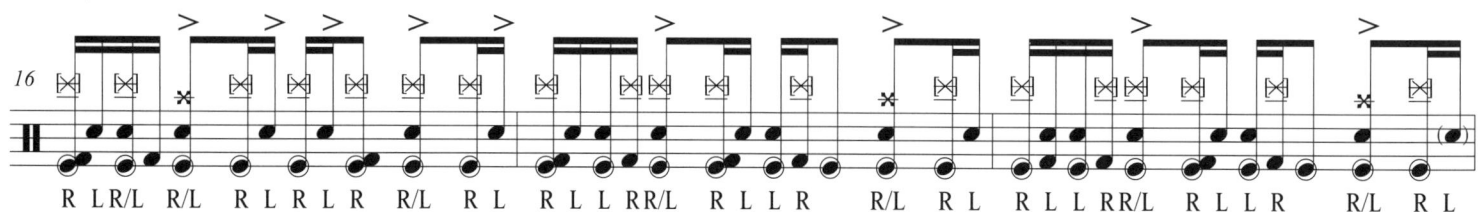

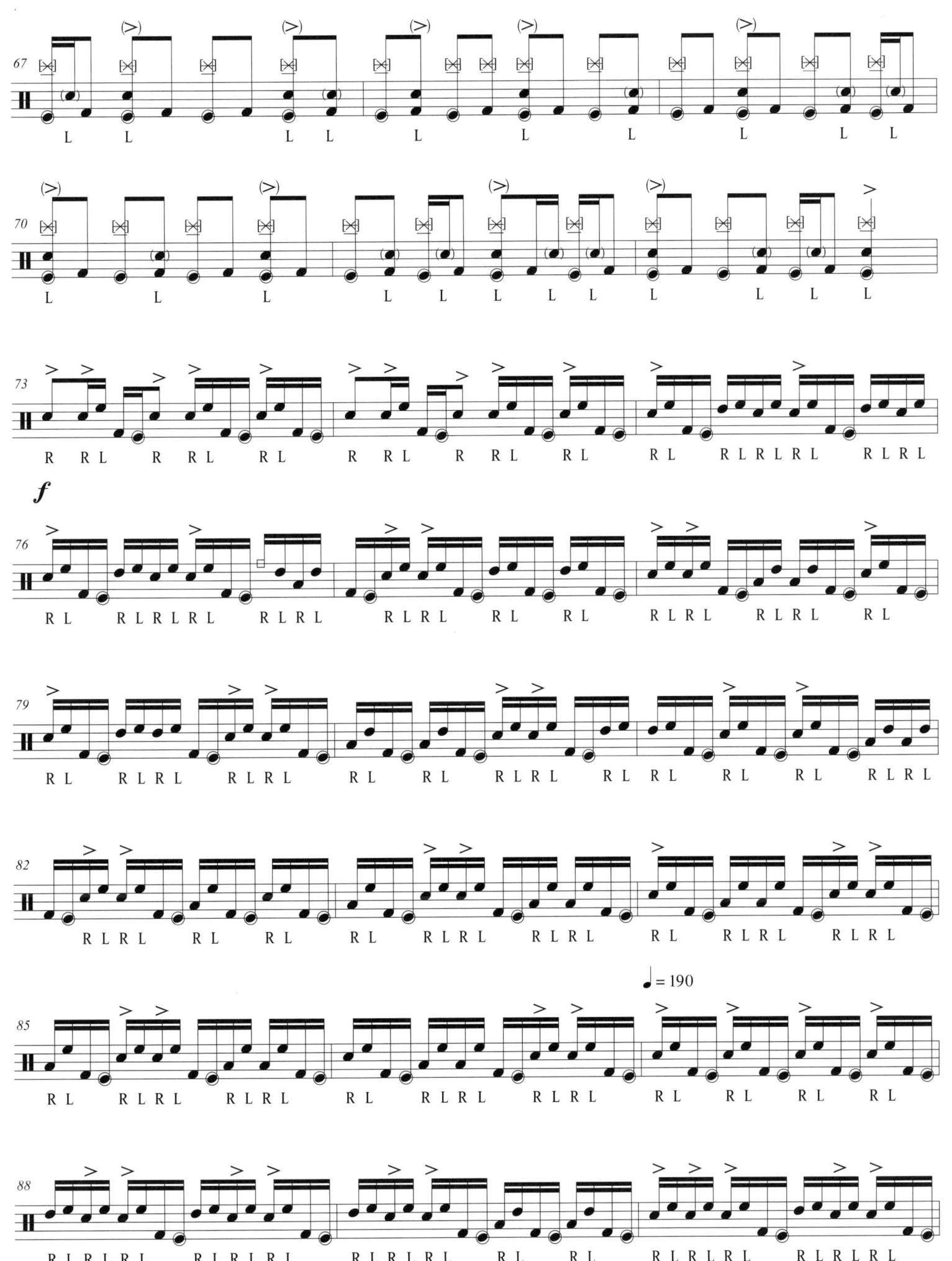

36 DRUM WARS | CARMINE'S SOLO

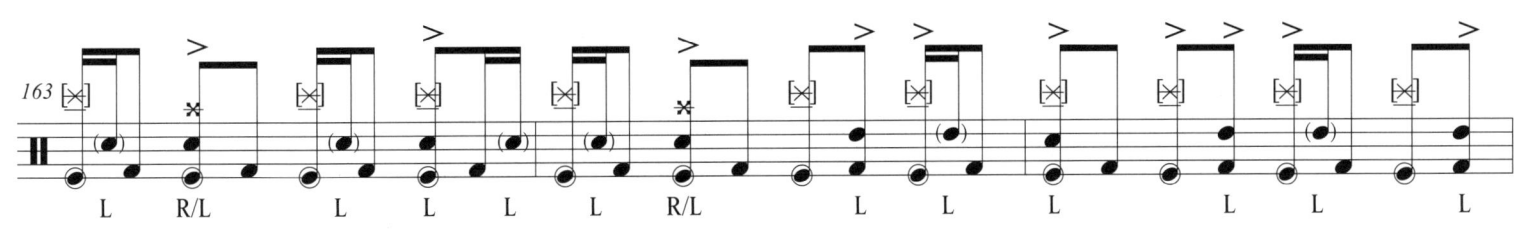
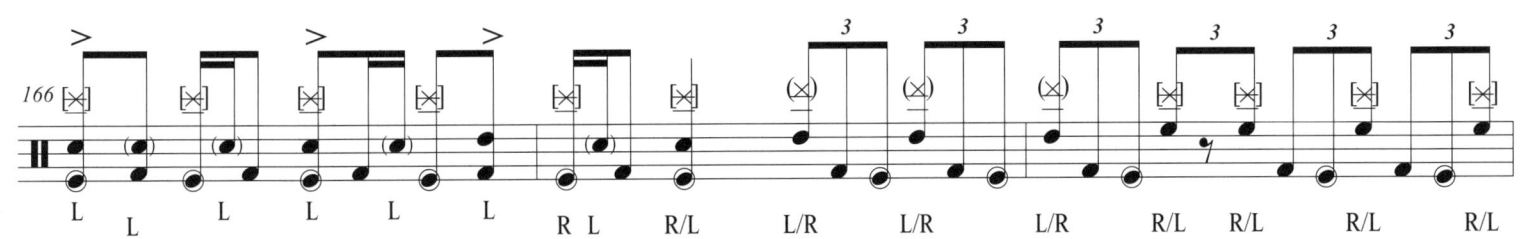
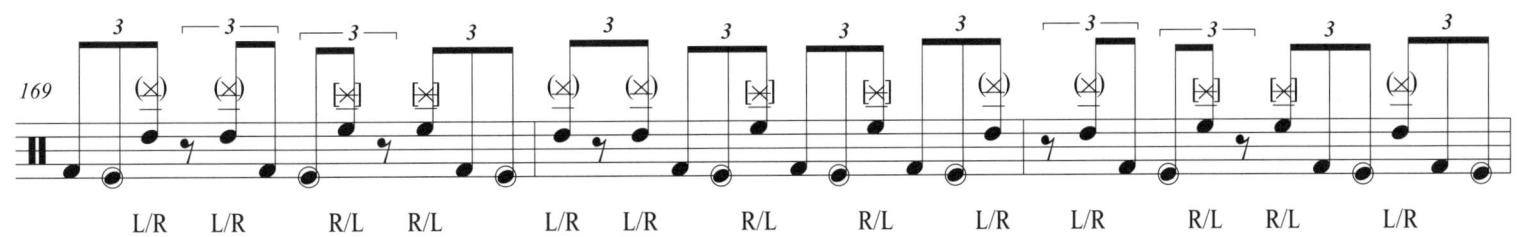
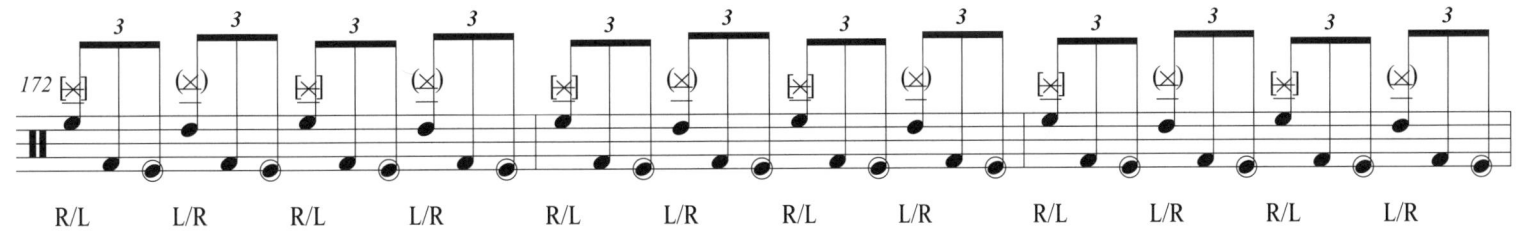
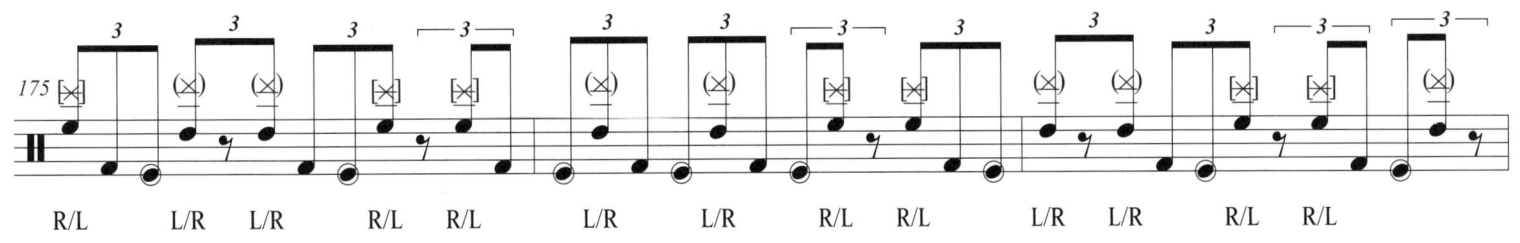

VINNY'S SOLO
Exercises and Examples

Notation Key

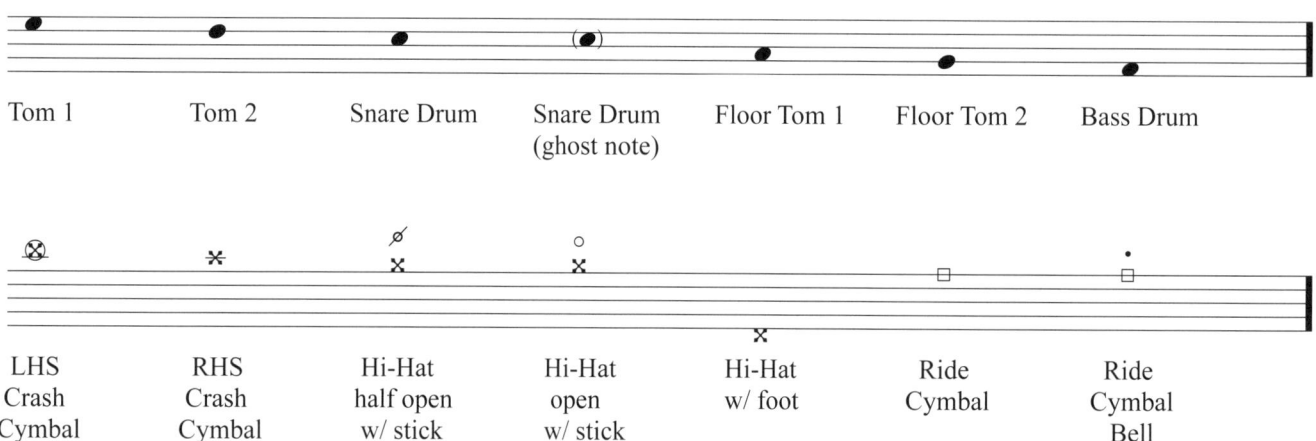

iNTRO GROOVE

This section begins at 29:24 (100% normal speed), at 20:23 (75% of the normal speed), and at 6:57 (50% of the normal speed).

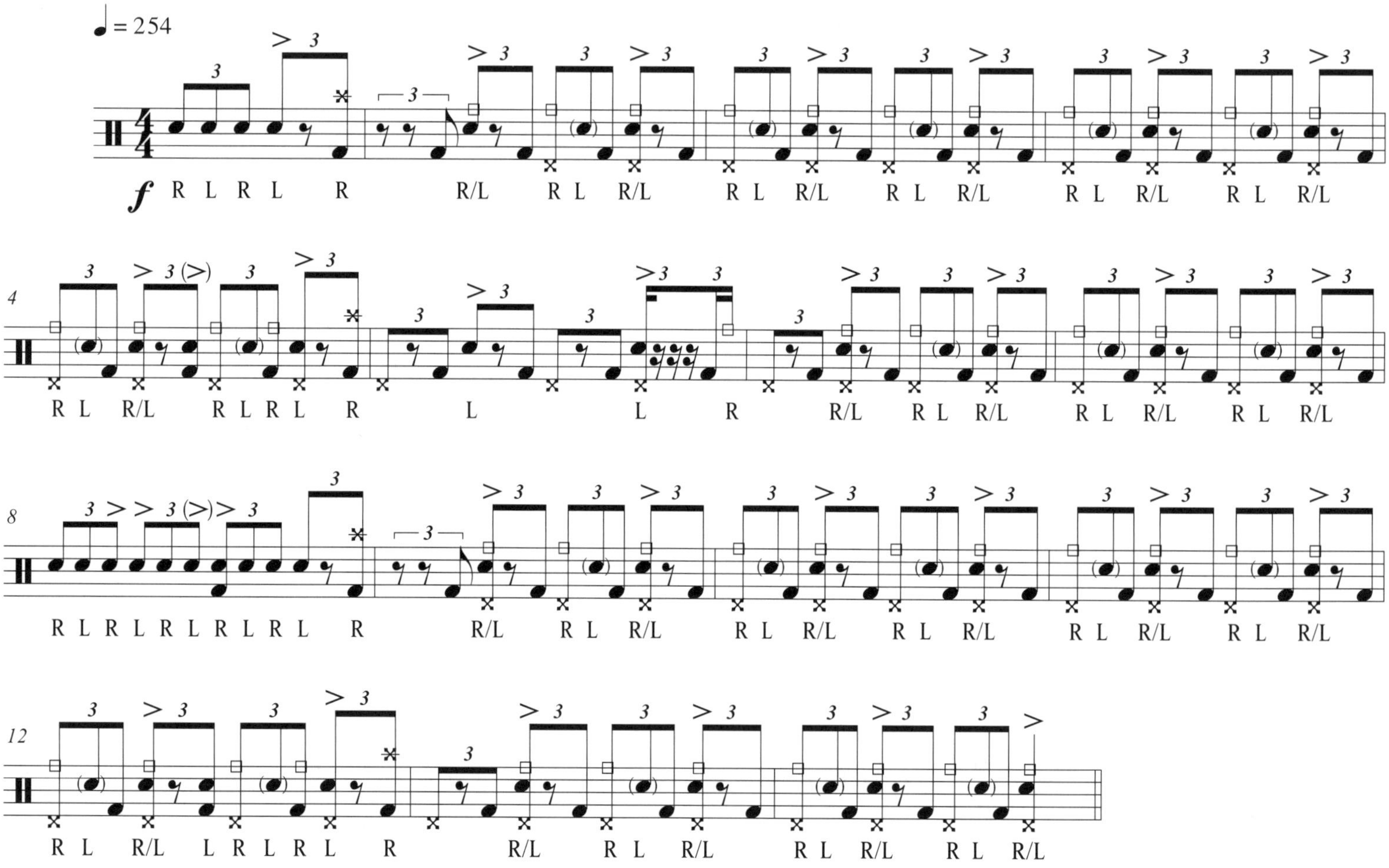

This shuffle groove is played on the ride cymbal, and is similar to Carmine's double-bass shuffle (but with the left foot on the hi-hat instead of the second bass drum).

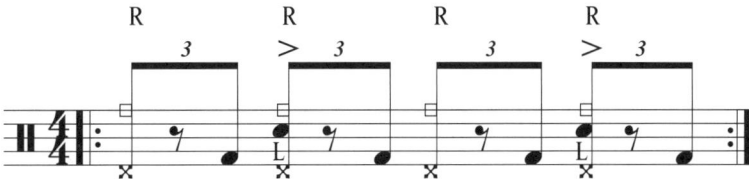

Adding ghost notes on the snare with the left hand creates the main groove of the introduction.

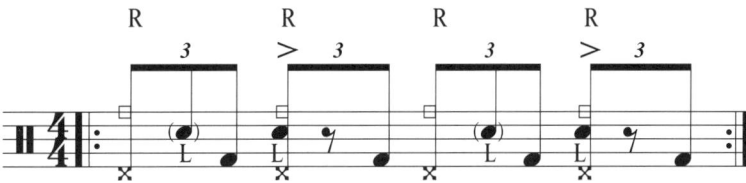

The following example is a variation of the main groove.

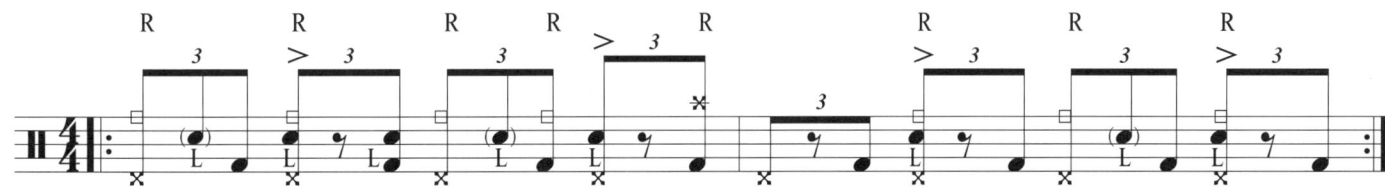

42 DRUM WARS | VINNY'S SOLO

SNARE DRUM PATTERNS

This section begins at 29:38 (100% normal speed), at 20:41 (75% of the normal speed), and at 7:25 (50% of the normal speed).

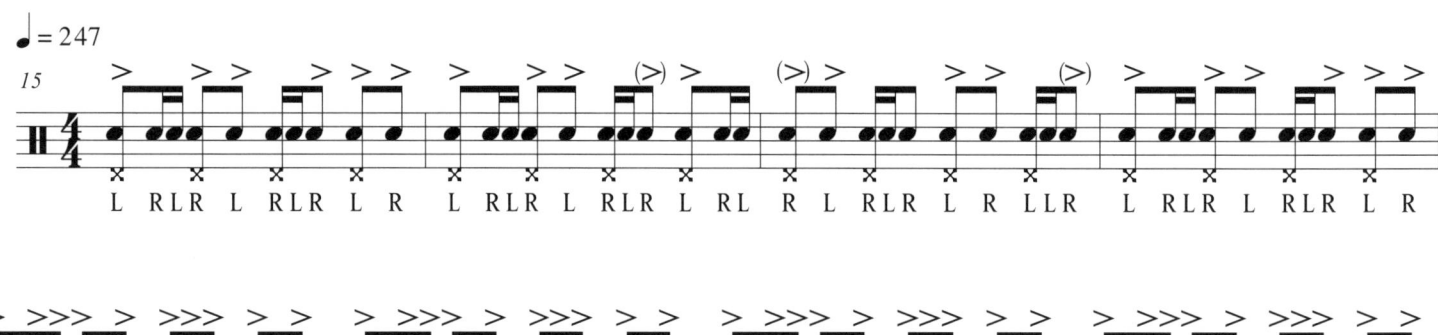

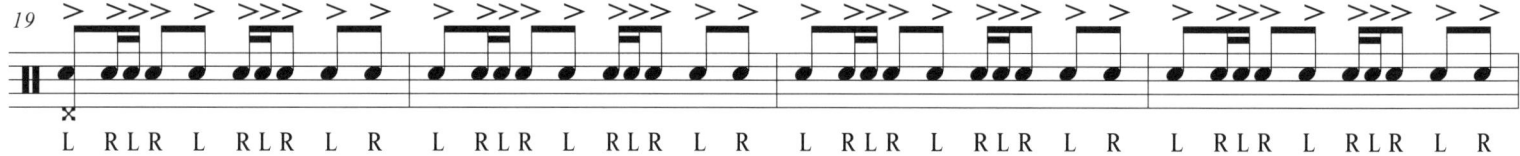

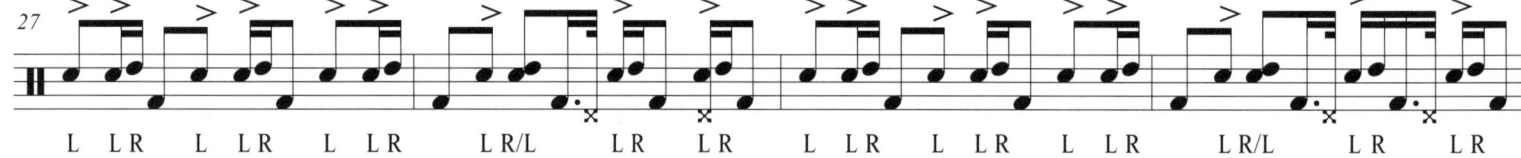

The section begins with this basic snare pattern.

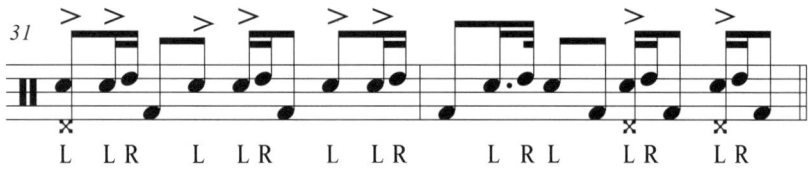

Adding quarter notes to the hi-hat looks like this.

Practice this exercise slowly and steadily. Speed will come with control.

Next, play the bass drum on the "&" of 1, and on beat 3 while accenting all snare notes. It is played double forte (ff) in the transcription.

By substituting a few bass drum notes for snare notes and moving the right hand to the tom, the following pattern is created.

The following phrase should be practiced slowly.

Playing the pattern above with quarter notes on the hi-hat is a great way to develop independence.

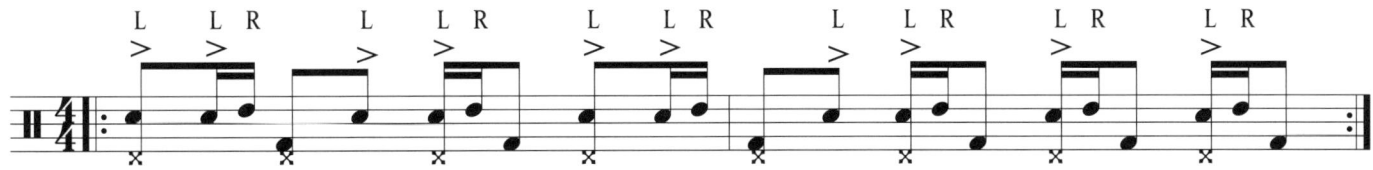

While playing the following snare pattern, practice alternating eighth notes between the hi-hat and bass drum. This pattern can be found often in the transcription.

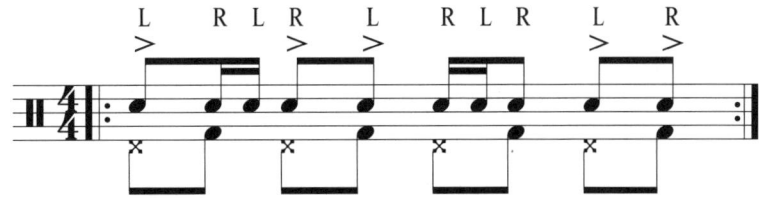

44 DRUM WARS | VINNY'S SOLO

SNARE DRUM PATTERNS

This section begins at 30:30 (100% normal speed), at 21:49 (75% of the normal speed), and at 9:07 (50% of the normal speed).

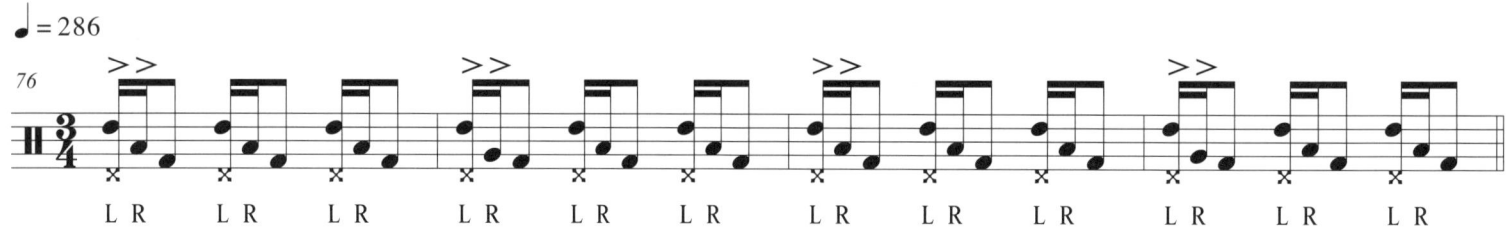

The pattern above is notated using sixteenth and eighth notes. As previously mentioned, the eighth-note triplet tends to take on this pattern at elevated tempos.

To start getting comfortables with the following pattern, practice the eighth-note triplet exercise slowly and evenly.

Now add the hi-hat with your foot.

Again, at faster tempos, the eighth-note triplets take on a sixteenth- and eighth-note pattern, as shown here.

Finally, practice the following pattern in 3/4, as represented in the transcription. Pay close attention to the accents.

TRIPLET RUFFS

This section begins at 31:01 (100% normal speed), at 23:31 (75% of the normal speed), and at 10:09 (50% of the normal speed).

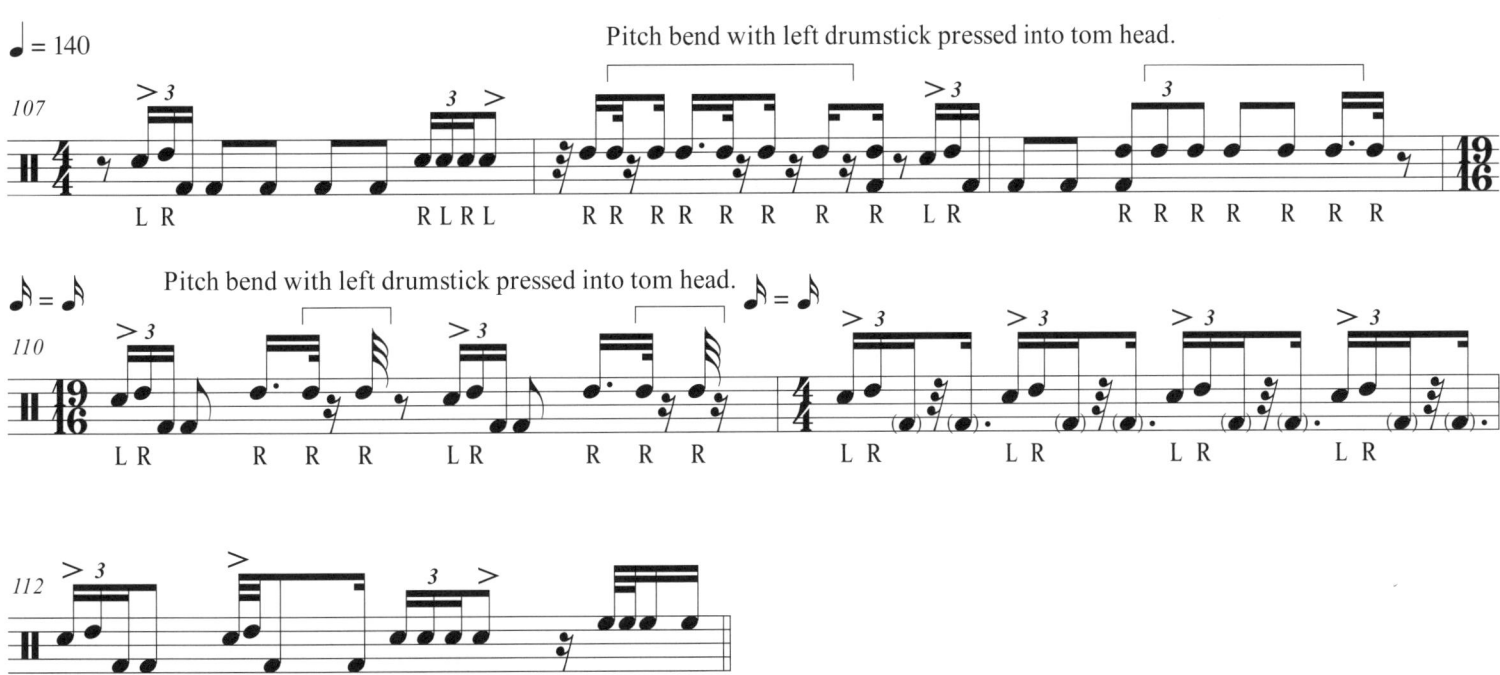

To help get comfortable playing the triplet ruff, practice the following pattern on the snare using alternate stickings. You can lead with either hand.

Next, while leading with the right hand, try breaking up the pattern by using the snare, toms, and bass drum. This pattern starts on the snare.

Now let's go in the opposite direction, starting with the floor tom.

As you can see, the transcription below shows the last two notes of the triplet ruff being played on the bass drum. This pattern leads with the left hand, and is a good exercise to help get your foot in shape. Remember to start slowly!

This next exercise combines elements of the previous triplet-ruff exercises. It will really help you become more fluid with the ruff pattern.

SIXTEENTH-NOTE GROOVE

This section begins at 31:19 (100% normal speed), at 22:54 (75% of the normal speed), and at 10:45 (50% of the normal speed).

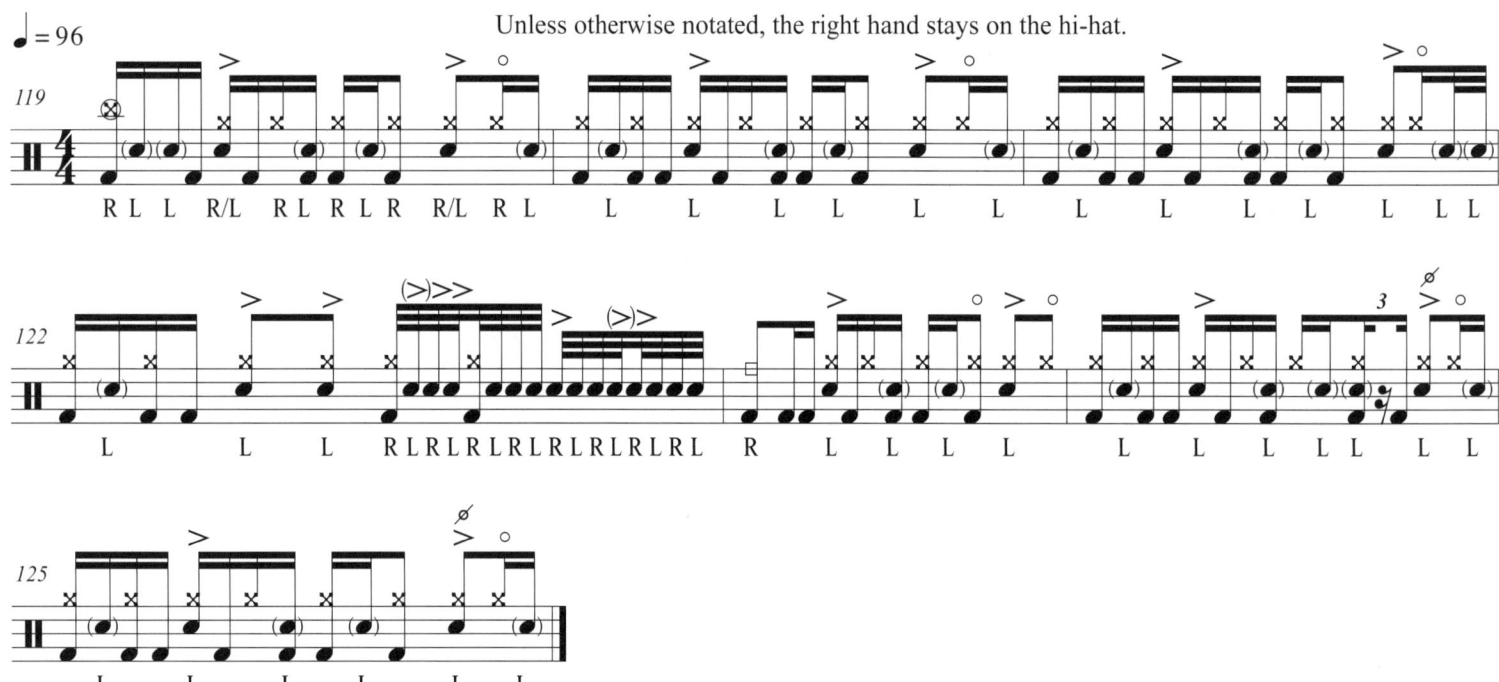

The basic groove consists of eighth notes played on the hi-hat, beats 2 and 4 on the snare, and a syncopated bass drum pattern.

Adding ghost notes on the snare adds a bit of flavor to the groove.

As always, practice slowly and steadily, and gradually build up to speed!

The big thirty-second note fill occurs in measure 122 of the transcription.

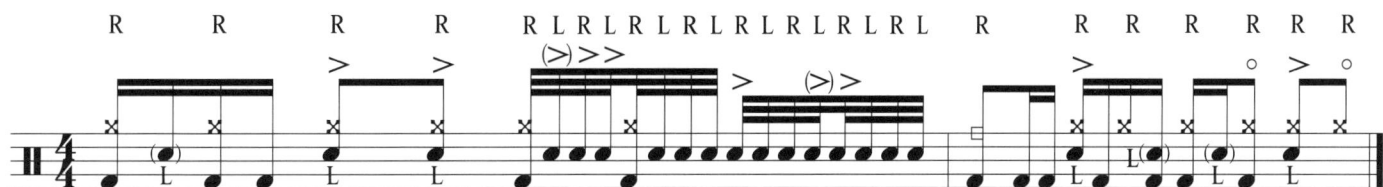

There are two thirty-second notes per sixteenth note—equal to eight thirty-second notes per quarter note. To get a feel for thirty-second notes, practice the following exercises, and pay close attention to the counting below the staff.

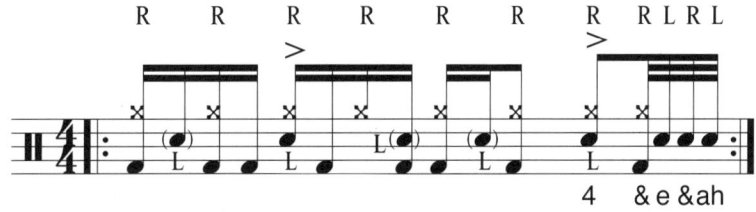

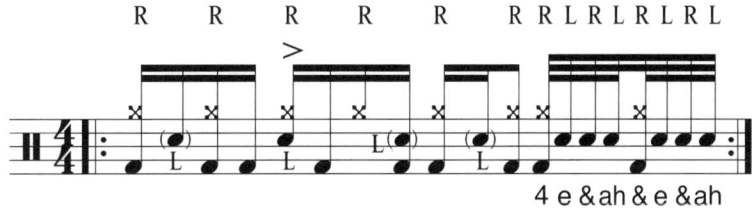

48 DRUM WARS | VINNY'S SOLO

GROUPS OF SEVEN-NOTE COMBINATIONS

This section begins at 32:37 (100% normal speed), at 24:39 (75% of the normal speed), and at 13:22 (50% of the normal speed).

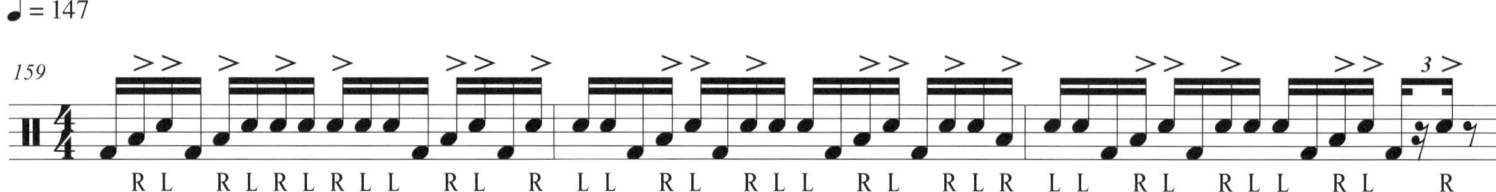

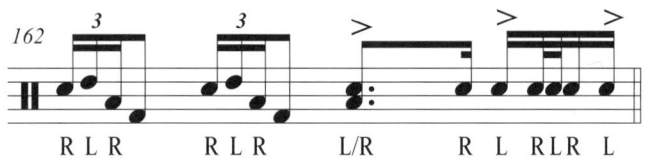

The phrase above begins on beat 3 of measure 159, and consists of sixteenth notes in a repeating pattern of seven notes. In order to get a feel for this rhythm, practice the following exercise.

Practice this pattern as well.

By playing both patterns consecutively and making the bass drum note of the second pattern a sixteenth note, the following pattern emerges.

Start slowly, and pay close attention to the accents!

PARADIDDLES AROUND THE DRUMSET

This section begins at 33:16 (100% normal speed), at 25:37 (75% of the normal speed), and at 14:41 (50% of the normal speed).

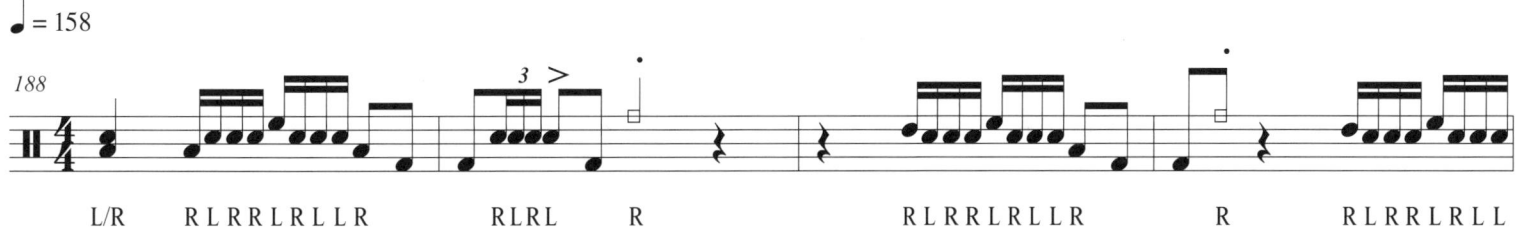

In order to get comfortable with this phrasing, we suggest you start on the snare.

Now break up the pattern by using the mounted toms and floor tom. Start on the floor tom with the right hand.

Another variation notated in the transcription starts with the right hand on the second tom.

GROUPS OF SIX-NOTE COMBINATIONS

This section begins at 33:27 (100% normal speed), at 25:47 (75% of the normal speed), and at 15:03 (50% of the normal speed).

♩ = 227

The groups of six, written as sixteenth notes, start on beat 3 of measure 198 above. To help develop confidence in performing these groupings, you can practice them as sixteenth-note triplets. The first two exercises distribute the groupings among the hi-hat, snare, and bass drum.

Now split the pattern up by using the floor tom, mounted toms, snare, and bass drum.

Writing the pattern using sixteenth notes, as it appears in the transcription, results in the following patterns. The 6/4 time signature allows the patterns to be repeated for practice.

DRUM WARS | VINNY'S SOLO

GROOVE WITH THIRTY-SECOND NOTES

This section begins at 33:49 (100% normal speed), at 26:16 (75% of the normal speed), and at 15:47 (50% of the normal speed).

Unless otherwise notated, the right hand stays on the hi-hat.

52 DRUM WARS I VINNY'S SOLO

The main groove is shown below and consists of eighth notes played on the hi-hat, ghost notes played with the left hand, and four thirty-second notes, each played on the "&" of beats 1 and 3.

The basic groove without the thirty-second notes looks like this.

To develop a feel for thirty-second notes, practice the following patterns.

Play the exercises slowly in order to execute the thirty-second notes cleanly. Make sure all subdivisions are played evenly, and refer to the solo video clips and MP3s to hear how they are interpreted.

Here is another variation of the main groove.

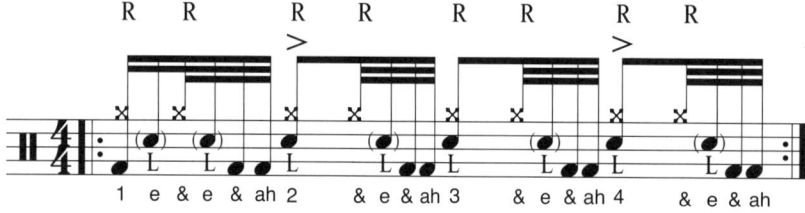

Here is how the groove looks without the thirty-second notes.

Practice the thirty-second note development patterns, and then add them to this basic groove. Remember, you must take your time when developing this rhythmic awareness.

DRUM WARS | VINNY'S SOLO 53

Vinny's Complete Drum Solo Transcription
Recorded Live in 2013

Before playing the following solo, please refer to the notation legend on page 40.

Transcribed by Eric Fischer

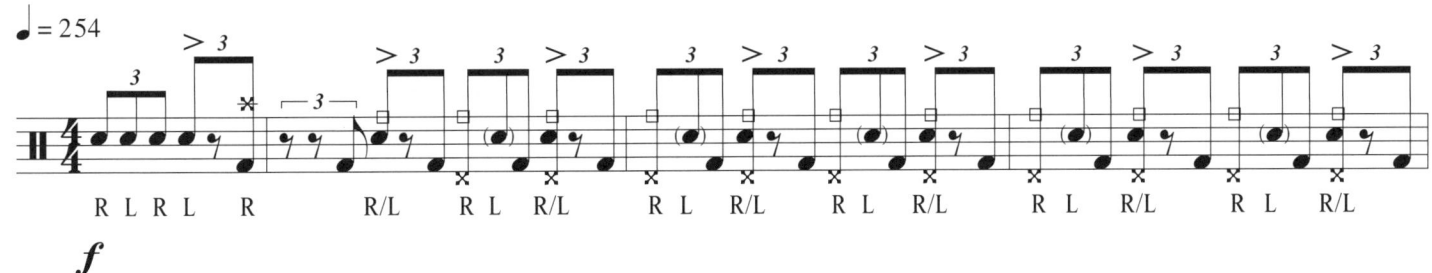
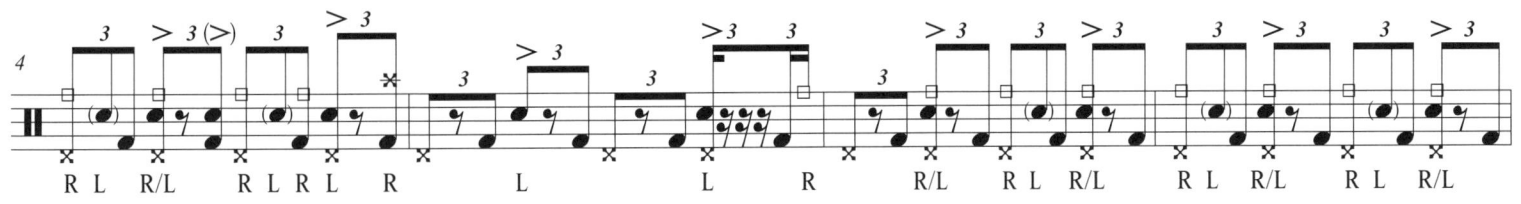
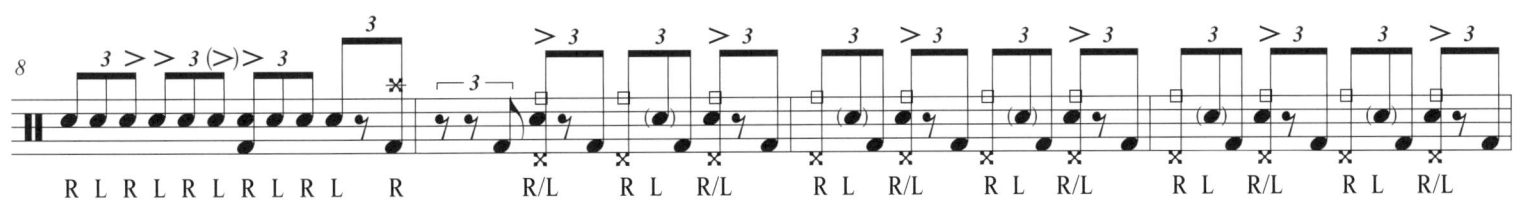
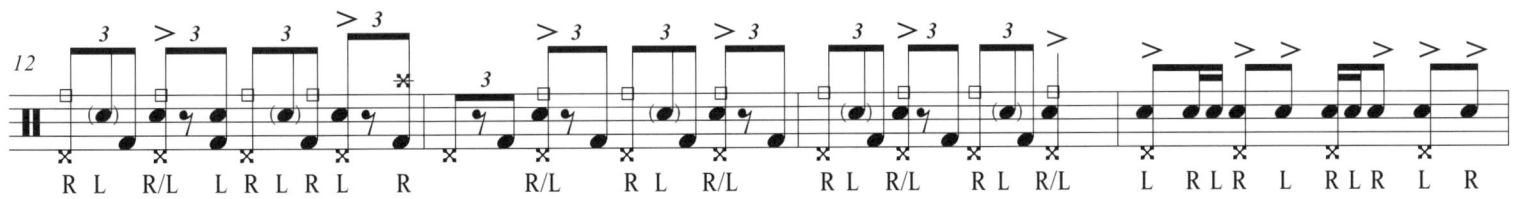
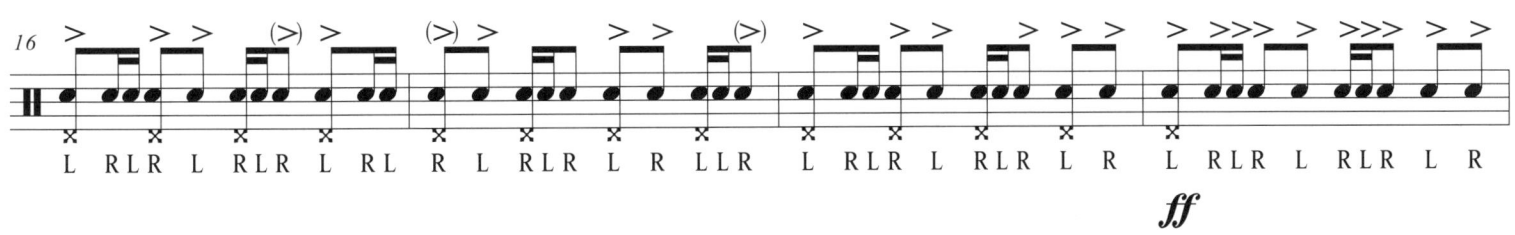

54 DRUM WARS | VINNY'S SOLO

56 DRUM WARS | VINNY'S SOLO

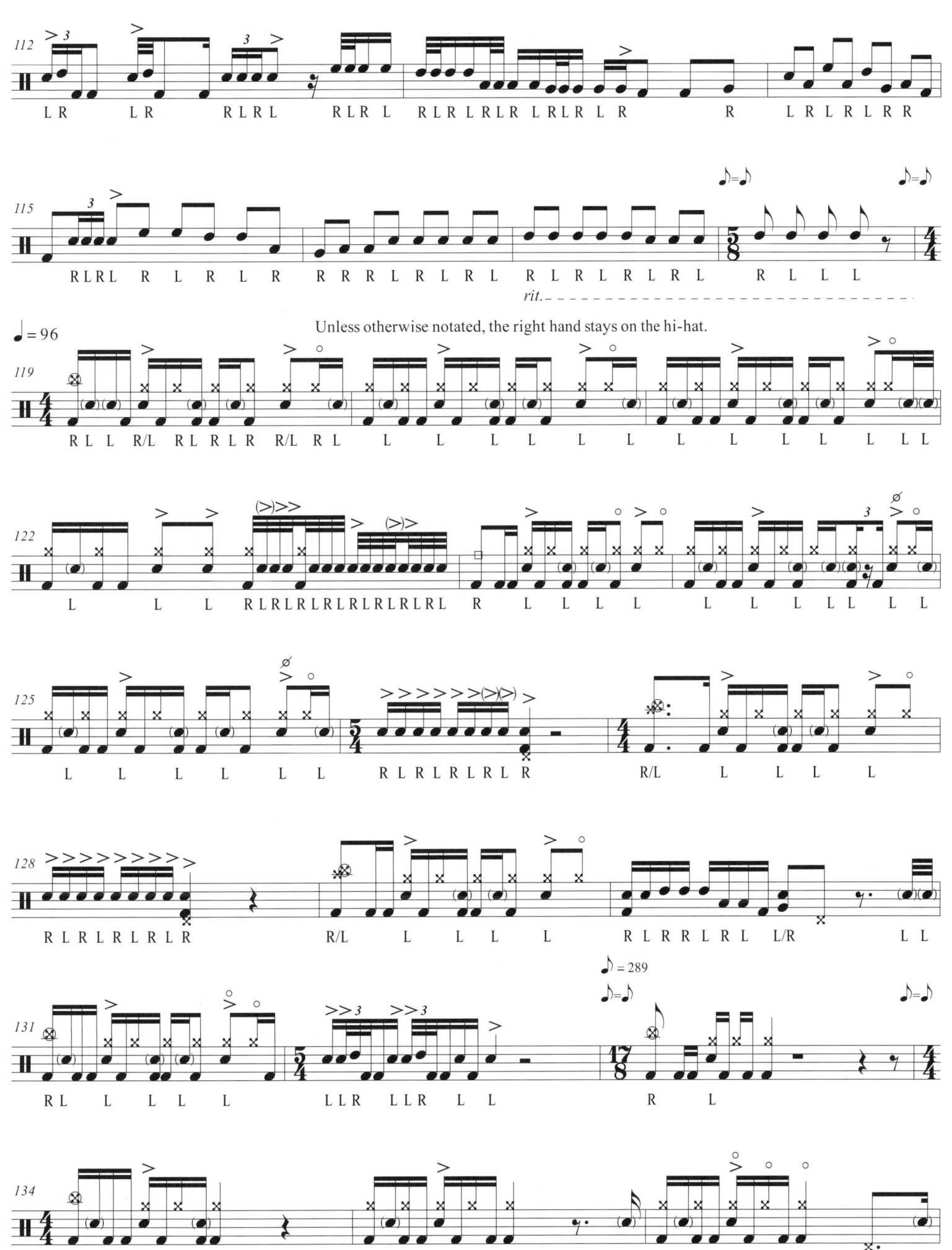

58 DRUM WARS | VINNY'S SOLO

DRUM WARS | VINNY'S SOLO

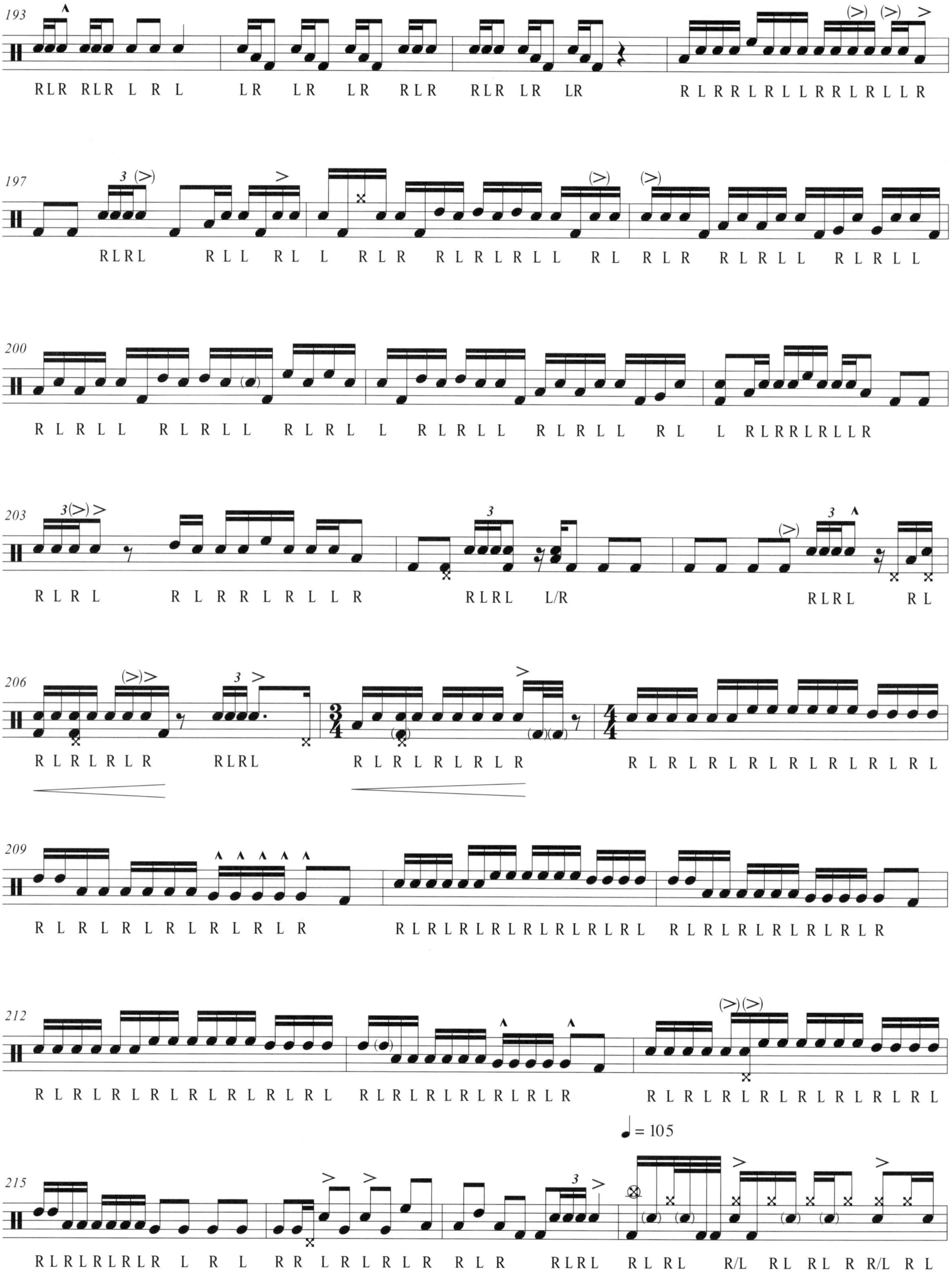
193
RLR RLR L R L LR LR LR RLR RLR LR LR R L R R L R L L R R L R L L R
197
RLRL R L L R L L R L R R L R L R L L R L R L R R L R L L R L R L L
200
R L R L L R L R L L R L R L L R L R L L R L R L L R L L RLRRLRLLR
203
R L R L R L R R L R L L R RLRL L/R RLRL R L
206
R L R L R L R RLRL R L R L R L R L R R L R L R L R L R L R L R L R L
209
R L R L R L R L R L R L R RLRLRLRLRLRLRLRL RLRLRLRLRLRLR
212
R L R L R L R L R L R L R L R L RLRLRLRLRLRLR R L R L R L R L R L R L R L R L
♩ = 105
215
RLRLRLRLR L R L R R L R L R L R R L R RLRL RL RL R/L RL RL R R/L R L

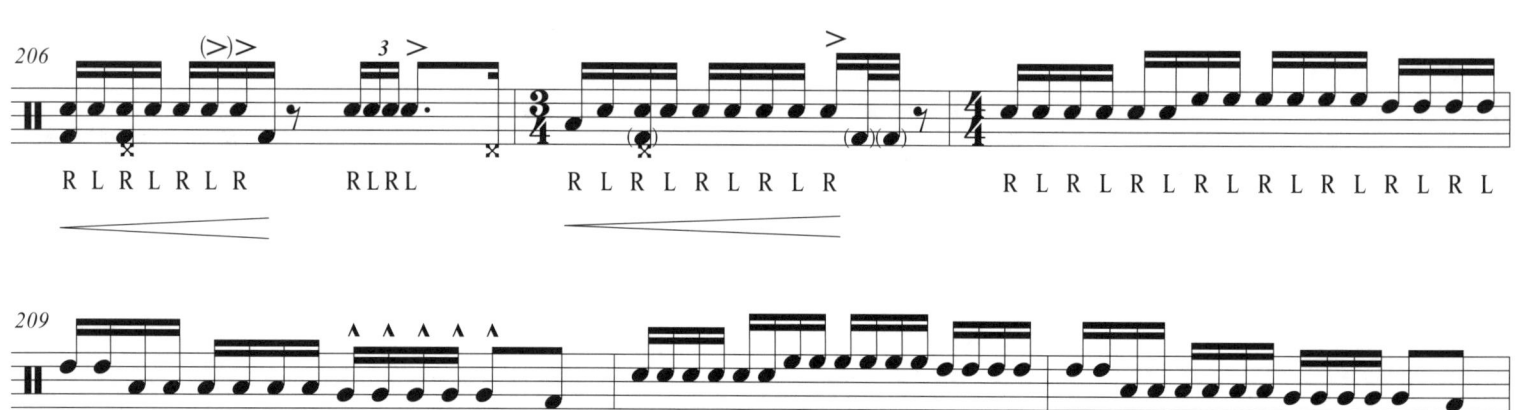

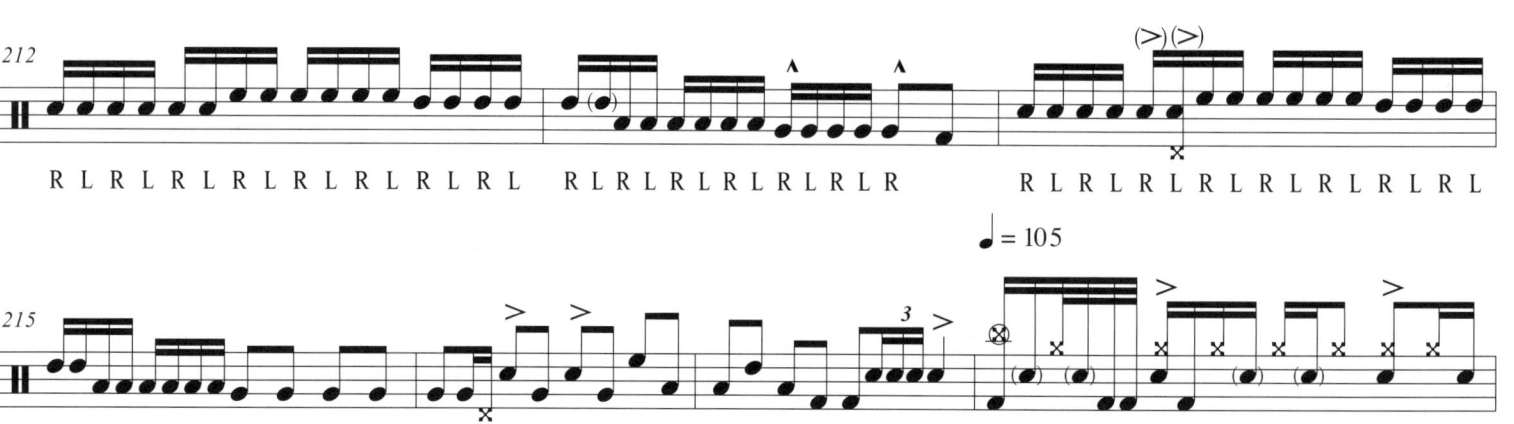

DRUM WARS | VINNY'S SOLO

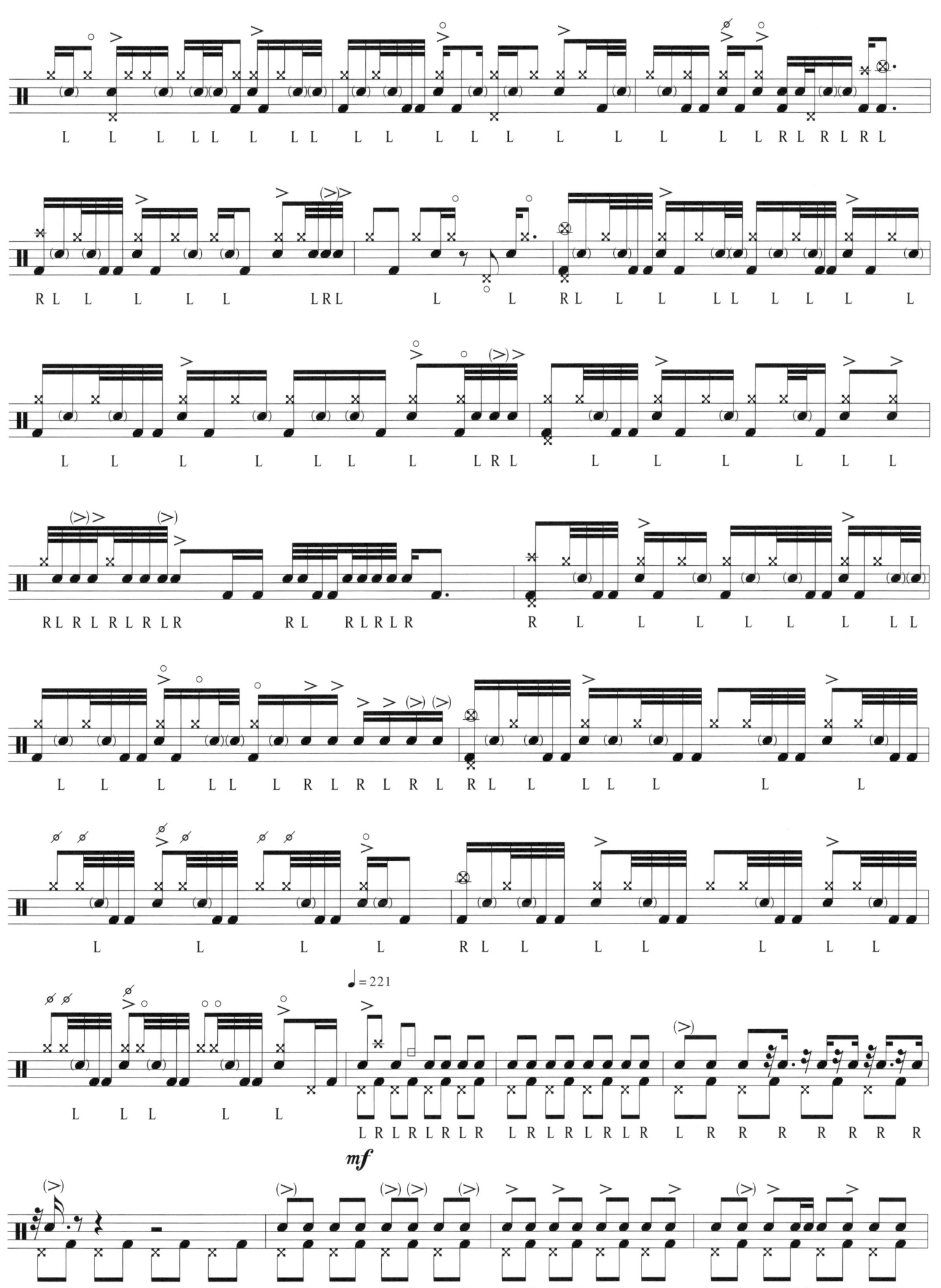

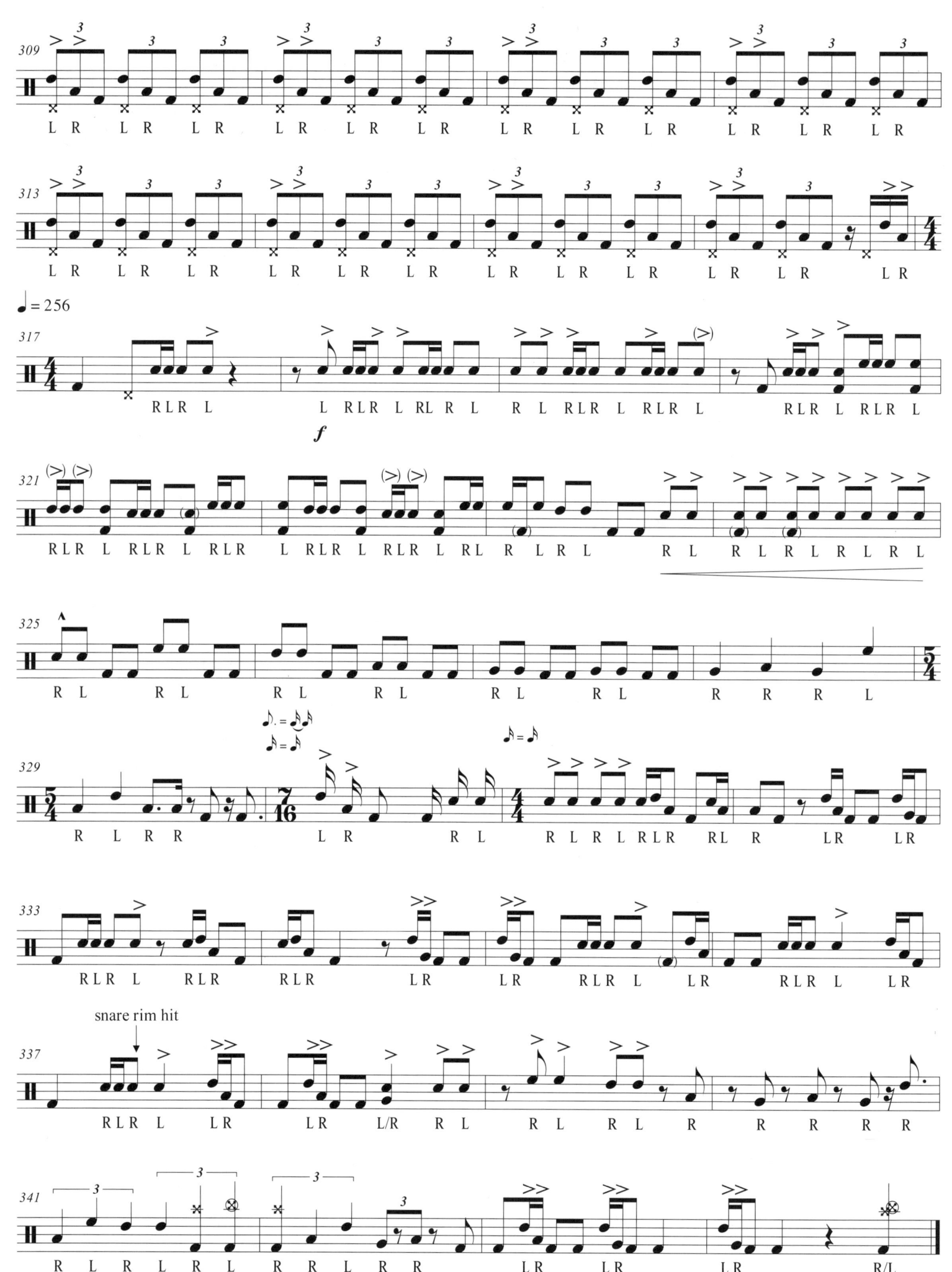